At Issue

Wave and Tidal Power

Other Books in the At Issue Series:

At Issue

Wave and Tidal Power

Louise I. Gerdes, Book Editor

GREENHAVEN PRESS
A part of Gale, Cengage Learning

Detroit • New York • San Francisco • New Haven, Conn • Waterville, Maine • London

GALE
CENGAGE Learning‑

Christine Nasso, *Publisher*
Elizabeth Des Chenes, *Managing Editor*

For more information, contact:
Greenhaven Press
27500 Drake Rd.
Farmington Hills, MI 48331-3535
Or you can visit our Internet site at gale.cengage.com

For product information and technology assistance, contact us at

Gale Customer Support, 1-800-877-4253
For permission to use material from this text or product, submit all requests online at www.cengage.com/permissions.

Further permissions questions can be e-mailed to permissionrequest@cengage.com.

Articles in Greenhaven Press anthologies are often edited for length to meet page require-ments. In addition, original titles of these works are changed to clearly present the main thesis and to explicitly indicate the author's opinion. Every effort is made to ensure that Greenhaven Press accurately reflects the original intent of the authors. Every effort has been made to trace the owners of copyrighted material.

Cover image copyright Debra Hughes 2007. Used under license from Shutterstock.com.

LIBRARY OF CONGRESS CATALOGING-IN-PUBLICATION DATA

Wave and tidal power / Louise I. Gerdes, book editor.
    p. cm. -- (At issue)
    Includes bibliographical references and index.
    ISBN 978-0-7377-4900-7 (hardcover) -- ISBN 978-0-7377-4901-4 (pbk.)
    1. Tidal power. 2. Ocean wave power. I. Gerdes, Louise I., 1953- II. Series: At is-sue (San Diego, Calif.)
    TC147.W375 2010
    621.31'2134--dc22
                                                                        2010027451

Printed in the United States of America
2 3 4 5 6   15 14 13 12 11

FD193

Contents

Introduction

The world's oceans, which cover more than 70 percent of the earth's surface, arguably are the largest potential power source in the world. The spinning of the earth combines with the heat from the sun to generate strong ocean currents and waves. The gravitational pull of the moon as it travels round the earth, as well as the gravity of the earth itself as it circles the sun, creates the ebb and flow of tides. Both forces create an enormous amount of kinetic energy, leading some commentators to claim that ocean energy is one of the largest untapped renewable energy resources on the planet. According to renowned oceanographer Jacques Cousteau, the power produced by the ocean is equivalent to 16,000 nuclear power plants. Moreover, unlike other renewable sources such as wind and solar power, the energy of currents, tides, and waves is available twenty-four hours a day, seven days a week. Water also is dense, which makes ocean energy more efficient than wind. In fact, some say the oceans could power the world.

Despite its enormous potential, wave and tidal energy represents only a small segment of renewable energy investment. Although the use of wave and tidal power is not new, ocean power is in its infancy as an energy industry. In the early 1970s, during the oil crisis of that decade, governments in Europe and the United States began to explore ocean energy as a renewable resource. While ocean energy projects received some support, once the immediate crisis abated, wind and solar power gained the greatest share of the renewable energy market. Despite urgent calls for renewable energy sources that produce little or no greenhouse gas emissions—an achievable goal for wave and tidal power—innovators of wave and tidal energy technology are hampered by greater economic, environmental, and regulatory hurdles than those faced by wind and solar projects in their early days. The increasing attention from and involvement of stakeholders, puts wave and tidal energy companies under incredible scrutiny. Indeed, one of the issues contested in the wave and tidal power debate is whether the nascent industry can surmount these hurdles.

Any new industry whose profits are unproven faces hurdles in being able to generate enough capital to meet significant start-up costs. According to the Electric Power Research Institute (EPRI), ocean energy could provide up to 10 percent of America's electricity. But in a 2007 article by Sandi Doughton for the *Seattle Times*, engineering professor Annette von Jouanne of Oregon State University (OSU) claims that ocean energy's "potential won't become a reality until the technologies mature." OSU is the nation's leading wave-power research center. In an effort to help the nascent ocean energy industry get off the ground, OSU offers companies the use of its wave-energy research and demonstration facility off the Oregon coast, where they can measure power output and collect data. OSU collaborates with the University of Washington, which studies tidal energy at the Northwest National Marine Renewable Energy Center. In fact, experts claim that the waters off the coast of Washington and Oregon are ideal for the generation of electricity from ocean energy technologies. According to von Jouanne, waves off the northwest coast could generate power 80 to 90 percent of the time, unlike wind farms, which can generate power for less than half the time. Wave and tidal energy entrepreneurs are optimistic that operational costs will drop once their industries gain market strength. EPRI ocean energy advocate Roger Bedard asserts that wind energy started out around 40 cents per kilowatt/hour and eventually dropped to 7 cents per kilowatt/hour. Because water is denser than wind, and waves and tides are more predictable, Bedard reasons, ocean energy potentially will cost even less than wind energy.

Another hurdle facing the wave and tidal power industry concerns its potential impact on the marine environment, which currently remains relatively uncertain. In David C. Holzman's 2007 article for *Environmental Health Perspectives*, John H. Rogers, energy analyst of the Union of Concerned Scientists, reports, "I haven't heard of any specific environmental concerns with [wave and tidal power] yet, but it's something we will continue to follow." Some environmentalists worry about the impact of wave and tidal power technologies on fish, marine mammals, and marine ecosystems. For example, there are concerns about the impact of wave and tidal technologies on gray whales migrating off the Pacific Coast. Wave energy devices could destroy kelp forests where migrating mothers and calves find shelter. Also, the noise from tidal turbines might interfere with whale migration. In addition, tidal turbines could attract curious marine mammals and injure or kill them. These turbines might also create "dead zones" that interfere with nutrient patterns. Finally, there are concerns about how wave technologies may interfere with local fishing industries.

Wave and tidal power industry leaders are nonetheless confident that such environmental concerns can be resolved with adequate study. "If you provide design engineers with the right data," claims Charles Brandt, director of the Pacific Northwest National Laboratory's marine sciences lab in a 2009 article by Les Blumenthal for the Tacoma, Washington, *News Tribune*, "they can build technology that will be environmentally sustainable." In fact, following a study that the shear and pressure differences of turbines negatively impacted fish in the Pacific Northwest's Columbia River, newly designed turbines reduced fish injuries by 98 percent. According to Mary McCann, a biologist and manager of environmental services at a consulting firm in Portland, Maine, speaking to Holzman, the problem is "How do you get projects in the water to collect information to answer these questions when you are supposed to have the answers first, in order to get approval to put them in the water?"

Indeed, wave and tidal power advocates assert, the biggest roadblock is regulation. Although most U.S. states and the federal government have renewable energy production goals and incentives, the cost of obtaining permission to test a prototype can take years and millions of dollars in studies. For example, according to Trey Taylor of Verdant Power, a company that is testing tidal turbines in New York's East River, the cost of obtaining the necessary permits made up more than 50 percent of their budget. "It took more than four years to get approval to put six turbines in the water," Taylor maintains in the *Environmental Health Perspectives* article by Holzman. According to Sean O'Neill, president of the Ocean Renewable Energy Coalition, a national trade association that supports and advocates on behalf of ocean energy companies, regulators should not treat emerging wave and tidal energy technologies the same way they treat utility-scale projects such as dams. These regulatory obstacles, he argues, force companies like Verdant Power to devote most of their capital to securing permits instead of developing new technology that ultimately will replace nonrenewable, greenhouse gas–emitting fossil fuels. "A sense of proportionality needs to be built into the process," O'Neill explains to Holzman. Rogers, of the Union of Concerned Scientists, agrees. An expensive part of the permitting process is the environmental impact study. Rogers maintains that study requirements should balance against the environmental impact of not pursuing renewable technologies, which would include the construction of more coal or other fossil fuel plants already known to cause environmental damage.

Whether wave and tidal power companies will overcome these hurdles and secure a significant portion of the renewable energy market remains hotly contested. The authors of the following viewpoints in *At Issue: Wave and Tidal Power* debate this issue as well as the potential of wave and tidal power, threats these energy sources may pose, and how best to regulate the industry. Despite concerns, wave and tidal energy entrepreneurs are optimistic. According to columnist Neal Peirce, writing on the potential of wave and tidal power for the *Seattle Times* in 2006, "One is tempted to liken energy competition to a David and Goliath story—new upstarts, struggling for capital and market acceptance, against the entrenched fossil-fuels industries whose political clout delivers them more than $25 billion in federal subsidies each year." Peirce believes that due to the economic and environmental impact of global warming, the renewable energy "Davids" likely will triumph. Whether wave and tidal energy innovators will, in fact, be victorious remains unknown.

1

Wave and Tidal Power: An Overview

World Business Council for Sustainable Development

The World Business Council for Sustainable Development (WBCSD) is a global association of corporate executives who promote sustainable development. Members share knowledge, experience, and best practices and advocate for sustainable development by working with governments and nongovernmental and intergovernmental organizations.

The energy found in the world's waves and tides has the potential to power the world. Indeed, nations worldwide are experimenting with new ocean-energy technologies. Tidal power technology uses the rise and fall of tides to power turbines placed at the mouths of bays and rivers. These barrages and tidal stream systems convert tidal energy into electricity. Buoy systems convert wave energy from oceanic waves into mechanical energy, which is then converted into electricity. Not only is this ocean energy renewable, it is more efficient and predictable than wind or solar power. As new technologies, however, wave and tidal energy systems must overcome significant obstacles such as high start-up costs, a challenging marine environment, and unknown environmental impacts. Nevertheless, as nations strive to meet renewable energy needs, interest in wave and tidal projects continues to grow.

World Business Council for Sustainable Development, "Harnessing Energy from the Oceans," Globe-net.com, May 30, 2008. Reproduced by permission.

Forever moving—our restless oceans have enough energy to power the world. As long as the Earth turns and the moon keeps its appointed cycle, the oceans will absorb and dissipate vast amounts of kinetic energy—a renewable energy resource of enormous potential. But harnessing this resource has proven more difficult than first thought. . . . [This article explores] how the power of the oceans might eventually find its place among other forms of renewable energy.

Many People Live Near Oceans

According to the United Nations, 44% of the world's population lives within 150 km of an ocean coast. In Canada and Australia the number is much higher at 80%. In the United States 53% of the population lives in close proximity to an ocean.

Thus it is only natural that many countries look to the oceans as a source of energy to be harnessed. How they seek to exploit this resource varies according to factors of geography and available technologies.

The two main forms of energy associated with our oceans are tidal power and wave power—born of the same source, but different in how they turn energy into electricity.

Tidal Power

Tidal power coverts the energy of tides into electricity utilizing the rise and fall of the ocean tides. The stronger the tide, either in water level height or tidal current velocities, the greater the potential for tidal electricity generation.

Tidal generators act in much the same way as do wind turbines, however the higher density of water (832 times that of air) means that a single generator can provide significant power at velocities much lower than those associated with the wind power generators.

Tidal power can be classified into two main types; Tidal Stream Systems and Barrages.

Barrages are similar to hydro-electric dams but are placed in an estuary bay or river mouth, where they act as barriers that create artificial tidal lagoons. When water levels outside the lagoon change relative to water levels inside, turbines in the barrages are able to produce electrical power. There are only three such structures in the world: the Rance River in France, Canada's Bay of Fundy, and Kislaya Guba, Russia.

Tidal stream systems make use of the kinetic energy of moving water to power turbines. This technology simply relies on individual turbines which are placed in the water column; moored to be suspended, floating or anchored to the ocean floor. As the tide flows in or out, electrical energy is produced as water moves through the turbine.

Wave energy is captured using buoys which generate mechanical energy as they oscillate vertically from wave motion.

Tidal power boasts several advantages over other types of renewable energy technology, because tides are more predictable and reliable than wind energy or sunny days for solar power. Tidal energy has an efficiency ratio of approximately 80% in terms of converting the potential energy of the water into electricity. Tidal stream system turbines are only a third the diameter of wind rotors of the same power output.

As with wind power, location is [an] important factor in terms of being able to harness the earth's natural energy. Tidal stream systems must be located in areas with fast currents where natural flows are concentrated between natural obstructions, for example at the entrances to bays and rivers, around rocky points or headlands, or between islands and other land masses.

Wave Power

Ocean surface waves are also a considerable source of energy potential, but energy that is not as restricted in terms of location as tidal energy systems. Typically wave energy is captured using buoys which generate mechanical energy as they oscillate vertically from wave motion.

Terminator devices extend perpendicularly to the direction of wave travel and capture or reflect the power of the wave. Water enters through a subsurface opening into a chamber with air trapped above it and wave action causes the captured water column to move up and down like a piston to force the air though an opening connected to a turbine.

A point absorber is a floating structure with components that move relative to each other due to wave action (e.g., a floating buoy inside a fixed cylinder). The relative motion is used to drive electromechanical or hydraulic energy converters.

Attenuators are long multi-segment floating structures oriented parallel to the direction of the waves. The differing heights of waves along the length of the device causes flexing where the segments connect, and this flexing is connected to hydraulic pumps or other converters.

Overtopping devices have reservoirs that are filled by incoming waves to levels above the average surrounding ocean. The water is then released, and gravity causes it to fall back toward the ocean surface. The energy of the falling water is used to turn hydro turbines.

Wave power varies considerably in different parts of the world, and wave energy can't be harnessed effectively everywhere. According to the Ocean Renewable Energy Group, a Vancouver based organisation that promotes the development of ocean energy in Canada, regions considered to have "good" wave energy resources are generally those found within 40 to 60 degrees of latitude, where the strongest winds are found. Wave-power rich areas of the world include the western coasts of Scotland, northern Canada, southern Africa, Australia, and the northwestern coasts of the United States.

Worldwide Projects

Ocean energy company Clean Current Power Systems estimates a potential global market for 67,000 Megawatts (MW) of tidal and wave action equipment worth $200 billion. At 20 cents/kW [kilowatt] hour, the market for tidal electricity could be $27 billion annually. According to Finavera [Renewables, a Vancouver-based renewable energy company], worldwide wave energy could provide up to 2,000 TW [trillion watt] h/year, 10% of world electricity consumption. It comes as no surprise then, that interest in ocean energy has been building momentum in the past few years as these nations scramble to meet renewable energy targets.

For instance, in November 2007, British company Lunar Energy announced that it would be building the world's first deep-sea tidal-energy farm off the coast of Pembrokshire in Wales. Eight underwater turbines, each 25 metres long and 15 metres high will provide electricity for 5,000 homes. Construction is due to start in the summer of 2008 and the proposed tidal energy turbines, described as "a wind farm under the sea", should be operational by 2010.

> *Worldwide wave energy could provide up to 2,000 TW [trillion watt] h/year, 10% of world electricity consumption.*

Plans for a ten-mile barrage across the River Severn, which could generate 5% of the UK's [United Kingdom's] electricity needs, are currently under development. According to the UK Sustainable Development Commission, a barrage across the Severn would produce clean and sustainable electricity for 120 years. This would have a capacity of 8,640MW and an estimated output of 17 terawatt hours a year.

Scotland boasts roughly 25% of the entire European Union's tidal power potential and 10% of its wave energy potential and could produce more than 1,300 megawatts by 2020, enough to power a city the size of Seattle. In 2007, Scotland announced $26 million worth of funding packages to develop marine power in the nation. So far $8 million has been procured to develop 3 MW of tidal power.

UK-based Marine Current Turbines is developing a tidal stream system off the coast of Ireland. The 1.2-megawatt turbine will be tested for 12 weeks before feeding power into the Northern Ireland grid where it will operate for up to 20 hours per day, producing enough electricity to power 1,000 homes.

Both Scotland and England are planning wave energy projects. Scotland will be developing a 3 MW array and England will be developing a 20 MW Wave Hub off the north coast of Cornwall, England. The Cornwall project will power up to 7,500 homes.

North American Projects

Canada has the world's longest coastline and has always been serious about harnessing ocean energy. In early 2008 the Government of Nova Scotia gave the green light to three tidal energy testing projects in the Bay of Fundy to help establish a permanent tidal energy farm. Irving Oil is also studying 11 potential sites in the Bay of Fundy to develop tidal energy farms.

The Government of British Columbia estimates there are more than 6,000 megawatts of potential wave energy that have been identified so far in the province and projects are already under way to develop wave energy systems. In 2006 Vancouver-based Clean Current Power Systems began developing a pilot tidal power project near Victoria to demonstrate the potential for tidal power.

Pacific Gas and Electric Company and Vancouver-based Finavera Renewables is developing America's first commercial wave power plant off the coast of Northern California. The plant is scheduled to begin operating in 2012, generating a maximum of 2 megawatts of electricity.

In March 2008, the U.S. Department of Energy [DOE] announced it would be offering up to $7.5 million in grants for hydro-kinetic energy such as wave and tidal power. The department is seeking partnerships with companies and universities to develop the technologies and plans to award up to 17 grants.

Portugal is planning the world's first commercial wave farm, the Aguçadoura Wave Park near Póvoa de Varzim. If successful, a further 70 million euro is likely to be invested before 2009 on a further 28 machines to generate 72.5 MW.

Despite the enormous potential of ocean energy, there remain many pitfalls . . . that have proven difficult to overcome.

The Challenges

Despite the enormous potential of ocean energy, there remain many pitfalls (if such a word can be used in a watery context) that have proven difficult to overcome, and which explain why ocean energy remains the least developed of all forms of renewable energy. Problems still exist regarding cost, maintenance, environmental concerns and our still imperfect understanding of how power from the oceans will impact on the world's energy infrastructure.

For example, turbines are susceptible to bio-fouling; the growth of aquatic life on or in the turbine. This can severely inhibit the efficiency of energy production and is both costly and difficult to remove. Turbines are also prone to damage from ocean debris.

In the Bay of Fundy, project developers are particularly concerned with ice floes the size of small apartments, and cobblestones the size of watermelons constantly being tossed across the Bay's terrain by the power of the Bay's water flows.

Turbines may also be hazardous to marine life and the impacts on marine life are still largely unknown, but concern is warranted.

Barrage systems are affected by problems of high initial infrastructure costs associated with construction and the resulting environmental problems. For example, independent research on the economics of building the proposed Severn Barrage in the UK revealed that, taking environmental costs into account, the structure could cost as much as $12 billion to create—$4 billion more than previously estimated.

Barrage impacts include a decrease in the average salinity and turbidity within a barrage, significantly altering associated ecosystems.

Wave power systems present their own set of challenges. Most electric generators operate at higher speeds, and most turbines require a constant, steady flow. Unfortunately wave energy is slow and ocean waves oscillate at varying frequencies.

The rough realities of the marine environment have also proven difficult to deal with, especially for companies seeking to remain cost-effective. Constructing wave devices that can survive storm damage and saltwater corrosion add to development costs.

Both ocean wave and tidal power have attracted growing interest from investors and power utilities looking for the next long-term play in renewable energy.

The Future

Modern advances in ocean energy technology may eventually see large amounts of power generated from the ocean, especially tidal currents using the tidal stream designs. The technology is still in its infant stage and most projects that exist or that are in project development stages are mainly pilot projects. But the promise remains.

"It's not as well-established as solar, thermal, wind and biomass, but [ocean power] shows a lot of promise," said Philip Jennings, professor of energy studies at Western Australia's Murdoch University.

"As the technology develops and becomes more affordable, which it will over time, we can continue to expand pretty much anywhere where there is an ocean," said Chief Executive Officer Phil Metcalf of Pelamis Wave Power.

The market potential for tidal power still remains unclear. . . . Sector analysts believe Initial Public Offerings (IPO) for wave and tidal power projects will be much harder to price than for comparable wind power projects, because wave firms cannot give exact estimates on the scale of benefits and few have technologies that are up and running.

Regardless, both ocean wave and tidal power have attracted growing interest from investors and power utilities looking for the next long-term play in renewable energy.

"Water covers more than 70 percent of the Earth's surface," said Andy Karsner, assistant secretary for energy efficiency and renewable energy at the DOE. "Using environmentally responsible technologies, we have a tremendous opportunity to harness energy produced from ocean waves, tides or ocean currents, free-flowing water in rivers and other water resources to . . . provide clean and reliable power."

According to Jennings ocean power could not match fossil fuels for electricity production but could be competitive with other forms of renewable energy.

2

Wave and Tidal Power Must Overcome Significant Challenges to Be Useful

Martin LaMonica

Martin LaMonica is a senior writer for the Green Tech blog on CNET.com, a media news site that covers current technology and its impact on human life.

Although wave and tidal power have the potential to generate a sizeable percentage of needed electricity, this new technology must overcome significant hurdles to become commercially viable. In fact, few wave and tidal power designs have actually been tested. While the time from prototype to commercial use has been shorter than the development time of wind power, wave and tidal power is still an immature industry, and start-up costs remain high. In addition, the marine environment is harsh, which has led to delays and high maintenance costs. The most significant challenge, however, is environmental. To ensure that marine life will be protected from turbine blades, companies must spend money to gather data on the potential impacts of projects. Interest in the nascent ocean industry nevertheless continues.

The fledgling ocean energy industry is awash in ideas for making electricity from moving water but it is still reaching for a toehold in the commercial world.

Greentech Media last week released a summary of an ocean energy report that forecasts great potential for wave and tidal energy.

Ocean power—a resource often located near large population centers—could ultimately generate 25 percent of today's total electricity usage, said report co-author Travis Bradford, president of the Prometheus Institute for Sustainable Development.

In the next six years, electricity production from the ocean could swell from just 10 megawatts now to 1 gigawatt a year, a $500 million market.

Before ocean power becomes an economic reality . . .
there are huge hurdles to overcome.

Huge Hurdles

Before ocean power becomes an economic reality, however, there are huge hurdles to overcome, including too many competing turbine designs, lengthy environmental permitting, costly installation, and, in many cases, a harsh working environment at sea.

Research in ocean energy is active, with most of it done in the U.K. [United Kingdom]. There are a number of pilot projects in the works which, if completed, would total 650 megawatts of electricity production. That's roughly the size of one coal or natural gas power plant.

But charting the course from prototype to grid-connected generator has proven tricky, according to a number of speakers at an [October 2008] event hosted by the UK Trade and Investment initiative, Flagship Ventures, and Greentech Media.

"The challenges have been greater and the timelines have all slipped. It hasn't been an easy ride so far," said Andrew

Mill, CEO of the U.K.'s New and Renewable Energy Center (NaREC). "Most of the devices to date haven't actually reached the water."

Many wave power machines are designed to capture the energy of the wave's motions through a bobbing buoy-like device. Another approach is a Pelamis wave generator, now being tested in Scotland and in Portugal, which transfers the motion of surface waves to a hydraulic pump connected to a generator.

Tidal power typically uses underwater spinning blades to turn a generator, similar to how a wind turbine works. Because water is far more dense than air, spinning blades can potentially be more productive than off-shore wind turbines for the same amount of space.

Because it's an immature industry, ocean power is more expensive than other renewables.

Renewable, but Expensive

In addition to being renewable, another key advantage of ocean power is that it's reliable and predictable, said Daniel Englander, an analyst at Greentech Media.

Although they can't generate power on-demand like a coal-fired plant, the tides and wave movements are well understood, giving planners a good idea of energy production over the course of a year.

Because it's an immature industry, ocean power is more expensive than other renewables. In the coming years, the costs are projected to go down to about the range of wind and solar today, according to Greentech Media. "But the fact that you know when the generator is going to spin gives you a lot more value," Englander said.

Developing Ocean vs. Wind Energy

Many people consider ocean energy to be roughly at the same stage that wind power was at in early 1980s: there were a number of competing turbine and blade designs, and the cost of wind power was far higher than it is now.

As the number of ocean generator types consolidates and components become standardized—as has happened in wind power—the costs of ocean power devices should go down.

There has been about $500 million invested in ocean power since 2001, mostly in the form of government research and some venture capital, according to Greentech Media. That's tiny compared to wind or solar; several solar start-ups have individually raised more than that in the past year [October 2007–October 2008].

The report's authors predict that venture capitalists will be investing in ocean power as they seek new green-technology areas.

Big energy companies have dabbled in ocean power as well. General Electric purchased a stake in Pelamis Wave Power, while Chevron and Shell have invested in ocean companies through their venture capital arms, Englander said.

One positive sign is that ocean power appears to be developing quicker than wind, said John Cote, a vice president at General Electric's financial services arm.

"The wind industry, their Valley of Death (from product prototype to commercialization) was much longer," Cote said. "The development of standards is happening much quicker in the marine industry."

Tough Sailing

But despite the optimism, life on the water is tough, according to executives at ocean power companies.

With almost no infrastructure around the industry, companies need to build a lot of their own equipment. To install and test devices, they have to hire expensive vessels, typically used for offshore drilling.

Ocean Renewable Power is testing two of its horizontal turbine design tidal machines in Maine and Alaska. It's working on a new design that uses composite materials instead of steel, which it hopes to finish by the end of year [2008] and test extensively next year.

While working in freezing temperatures and 30-mile-per-hour winds in the Bay of Fundy off the Maine coast, it found that "everything that can go wrong, will go wrong," said Ocean Renewable Power CEO Chris Sauer.

Most of the failures were related to weather and marine conditions and equipment problems. "As a start-up, we have to make our own instrumentation systems put together on the cheap," he said.

New York City's East River, meanwhile, is the test site for another tidal power installation being led by Verdant Power, which makes underwater turbines that get energy from changing currents.

In the space of three weeks, all six turbines being tested failed the same way—a mechanical problem in the connections point between the blade and hubs, said Ronald Smith, Verdant Power's CEO.

Another big potential cost for ocean power devices is operations and maintenance.

Environment, Operations, and Maintenance

But the biggest hurdles with the project have been environmental concerns, he said.

Regulators want to make sure that fish, or other marine life, will not be killed in the blades. The company has equipped its devices with acoustic and other sonar devices to gather data for regulators, Smith said.

Another big potential cost for ocean power devices is operations and maintenance. Simply getting vessels—and staff—to service machines can be expensive, making the "survivability" of ocean energy gear a top priority.

Executives at the panel predicted that ocean power installations in the future will be several units, rather than one large device. For example, Ocean Renewable Power's 250-kilowatt modules can be stacked on top of each other, so if one machine fails, the entire operation isn't taken offline.

Even relatively successful companies—like Wavebob, which is set to build a 250-megawatt ocean power installation in Ireland—are doing software simulations, environmental reviews, and additional engineering to increase the odds of success.

"We're stopping on the edge of commercialization and taking two steps backward," said Derek Robertson, the general manager of the company's North American business. "We're investing in detailed operations and systems engineering process to retire risk."

3

Tidal Turbines Offer Advantages Compared with Nuclear and Fossil Fuels

Michael Maser

At the time of this writing, Michael Maser was media spokesperson for Blue Energy Canada Inc., a clean energy technology company that promotes the commercial use of a vertical axis hydro turbine for converting tidal currents into renewable electricity.

Tidal turbines—resembling underwater windmills—convert energy from tidal currents into electricity. This type of tidal power has the potential to produce as much electricity as nuclear or fossil fuels. Seawater is dense and therefore has more energy potential than does wind. Additionally, strong tidal currents create water velocity in certain areas of the world. While barrages that dam bays and estuaries are a proven tidal power technology, they are expensive to build and maintain, and they alter the environment. Underwater turbines, by contrast, are less costly and have little environmental impact. Tidal turbines produce no pollution or greenhouse gas emissions and pose no threat to the environment. Therefore they are endorsed by environmental organizations as an alternative to fossil fuels.

Twice each day, thanks to a gravitational pull on earth from our rotating moon, the world's oceans produce powerful water currents and rising and falling tides. Humans have

Michael Maser, *Tidal Energy—a Primer*, Richmond, BC: Blue Energy Canada, Inc., 2009. Reproduced by permission.

studied and exploited the tremendous power of the tides for millennia, including harnessing tidal power in 10th century dams to turn millwheels for grinding flour. Forty years ago, the first tidal dams were constructed to convert tidal power into electricity. One of the first such tidal dams was constructed on Canada's Bay of Fundy, where tides rise by as much as 12 metres (45 feet). Now, new energy technologies (NOT dams) that generate electricity from tidal currents could help produce as much reliable (Firm) electricity as the largest hydroelectric dams or nuclear and fossil fuel generating stations, without producing greenhouse gases or harming the environment.

The Advantages of Tidal Energy

The basic science of earth's tidal forces confers enormous advantages on this potential resource, namely:

- The earth's tides are a source of renewable power that is free, reliable (FIRM), and predictable years in advance (for ease of integrating with existing energy grid).

- By virtue of the basic physical characteristics that accrue to seawater, namely, its density (832 times that of air) and its non-compressibility, this medium holds unique, 'ultra-high-density' potential (in comparison with other renewables, and wind, especially) for generating renewable energy. This potential is *additionally amplified* when volume and flow rates present in many coastal locations worldwide are factored in. For example, a passage of seawater flowing with a velocity of 8 knots [1 knot = 1 nautical mile/hour or 1.15 statute miles/hour or 1.8 km/hour] has a wind-speed equivalent force of approx 390 km/hour or 230 miles/hour.

First-Generation, Barrage-Style Tidal Power

The oldest technology to harness tidal power for energy generation involves building a dam or a barrage, across a bay or estuary that has large differences in elevation between high and low tides. Water retained behind a dam at high tide generates a power head sufficient to generate electricity as the tide ebbs and water released from within the dam turns conventional turbines.

Though the American and Canadian governments considered constructing ocean dams to harness the power of the Atlantic tides in the 1930s, the first commercial-scale tidal generating barrage rated at 240 MW [megawatts] was built in La Rance [France]. This plant continues to operate today as does a smaller plant constructed in 1984 with the Annapolis Royal Tidal Generating Station in Nova Scotia, rated at 20 megawatts (enough power for 4,500 homes). One other tidal generating station operating today is located near Murmansk on the White Sea in Russia, rated at 0.5 megawatts.

Though they have proven very durable, barrage-style power plants are very expensive to build and are fraught with environmental problems from the accumulation of silt within the dam catchment area (requiring regular, expensive dredging). Accordingly, *engineers no longer consider barrage-style tidal power feasible for energy generation.*

Engineers have recently created two new kinds of devices to harness the energy of tidal currents ... and generate renewable, pollution-free electricity.

Second-Generation Tidal Current Power

Engineers have recently created two new kinds of devices to harness the energy of tidal currents (AKA 'tidal streams') and generate renewable, pollution-free electricity. These new devices may be distinguished as *Vertical-axis* and *Horizontal-axis* models, determined by the orientation of a subsea, rotating shaft that turns a gearbox linked to a turbine with the help of large, slow-moving rotor blades. Both models can be considered a kind of underwater windmill. While horizontal-axis turbine prototypes are now being tested in northern Europe (the UK [United Kingdom] and Norway) a vertical-axis turbine has already been successfully tested in Canada. Tidal current energy systems have been *endorsed by leading environmental organizations*, including Greenpeace, the Sierra Club of British Columbia and the David Suzuki Foundation as having "the lightest of environmental footprints," compared to other large-scale energy systems.

Tidal current energy generators are fueled by the renewable and free forces of the tides, and produce no pollution or greenhouse gas emissions.

Environmental Advantages

Like the ocean dam models of France, Canada and Russia, vertical and horizontal-axis tidal current energy generators are fueled by the renewable and free forces of the tides, and produce no pollution or greenhouse gas emissions. As an improvement on ocean dam models, however, the new models offer many additional advantages:

- because the new tidal current models do not require the construction of a dam, they are considered much less costly.

- because the new tidal current models do not require the construction of a dam, they are considered much more environmentally-friendly.

- because the new tidal current models do not require the construction of a dam, further cost-reductions are realized from not having to dredge a catchment area.

- tidal current generators are also considered more efficient because they can produce electricity while tides are ebbing (going out) *and* surging (coming in), whereas barrage-style structures only generate electricity while the tide is ebbing.

- Vertical-axis tidal generators may be stacked and joined together in series to span a passage of water such as a fiord and offer a transportation corridor (bridge), essentially providing two infrastructure services for the price of one.

- Vertical-axis tidal generators may be joined together in series to create a 'tidal fence' capable of generating electricity on a scale comparable to the largest existing fossil fuel-based, hydroelectric and nuclear energy generation facilities.

- Tidal current energy, though intermittent, is predictable with exceptional accuracy many years in advance. In other words, power suppliers will easily be able to schedule the integration of tidal energy with backup sources well in advance of requirements. Thus, among the emerging renewable energy field, tidal energy represents a much more reliable energy source than wind, solar and wave, which are not predictable.

- present tidal current, or tidal stream, technologies are capable of exploiting and generating renewable energy in many marine environments that exist worldwide. Canada and the US, by virtue of the very significant tidal current regimes on its Atlantic and Pacific coastlines—proximal to existing, significant electro-transportation infrastructure—is blessed with exceptional opportunities to generate large-scale, renewable energy for domestic use and export.

Tidal Energy Prototypes

Vertical-axis tidal turbine

A Canadian company—Blue Energy Canada Inc.—has completed six successful prototypes of its vertical-axis 'Davis Hydro Turbine,' named after its inventor, the late Barry Davis. Barry Davis trained as an aerospace engineer, working on the renowned Canadian Avro 'Arrow' project, then on the equally-remarkable 'Bras D'Or' hydrofoil project of the Canadian Navy. Barry then decided to apply his knowledge of hydrodynamics in creating a tidal energy generator. Barry received support from the Canadian National Research Council and successfully tested 5 turbine prototypes in the St. Lawrence Seaway and on the eastern seaboard. Blue Energy is presently raising funds for a commercial demonstration project of the Davis Hydro Turbine.

Horizontal-axis tidal turbine

Although they were proposed during the oil crisis of the 1970s, the first tidal turbines began operating in the mid-1990s when a 15-kilowatt horizontal-axis tidal turbine was installed in Loch Linnhe on the west coast of Scotland, north of Glasgow. Now, two companies in the United Kingdom are planning to initiate horizontal-axis tidal turbine demonstration projects while another demonstration project has begun off the coast of Norway. A US company has also designed a working prototype. Horizontal-axis tidal turbines closely resemble wind turbines, except that the turbine and blades are completely submerged in water.

Is Tidal Energy Expensive?

No, tidal energy power systems are expected to be very competitive with other conventional energy sources, and excellent cost advantages arise from there being no pollution or environmental expenses to remediate nor are their fuel expenses (the kinetic energy of tidal currents is free). Further, ongoing maintenance costs are expected to be modest, as they are with other large-scale marine infrastructures, e.g. bridges, ships, etc., and a non-polluting tidal energy regime will qualify for valuable carbon offset credits. A 2002 feasibility report on tidal current energy in British Columbia [BC] by Triton Consultants for BC Hydro stated, "Future energy costs are expected to reduce considerably as both existing and new technologies are developed over the next few years. Assuming that maximum currents larger than 3.5 m/s can be exploited and present design developments continue, it is estimated that future tidal current energy costs between 5¢/kWh and 7¢/kWh are achievable."

American President John F. Kennedy, a champion of a large-scale barrage-style tidal power project . . . , envisioned a 'fossil-fuel-free energy future' on the Atlantic seaboard.

Recent Research

New technologies to harness tidal current power and generate electricity, though not yet available commercially, are being tested and investigated by researchers. So, too, are researchers beginning to assess the generating potential of regional tidal current energy regimes. The following points underscore the exciting potential of this emerging resource:

1. An engineering research report released by the University of Southampton [U of S], UK, 2003, describes marine current turbines as a more effective and predictable energy resource than wind turbines, with the potential to access an estimated four times more energy. Dr. AbuBakr S. Bahaj of the Sustainable Energy Research Group, U of S, asserts, "a tidal current turbine rated to work in a flow between 2 to 3 metres per second in seawater can typically access four times as much energy per rotor swept area as a similarly rated power wind turbine." Dr. Bahaj adds, "the potential of the electricity that can be produced from the resource is high. For example, *our current estimate of such a potential for only one site, the races of*

the Channel Islands, indicates that this will be about the same as the electricity produced by three Sizewell B nuclear power stations [= 3 GW (gigawatts)]." The Department of Civil Engineering (CEE) and the School of Engineering Sciences (SES) at the U of S were recently awarded £215,000 by the Engineering and Physical Sciences Research Council (EPSRC) to research the development of turbines to generate power as tides ebb and flow.

2. British Columbia has taken the first small (and conservative) steps to estimating the energy-generating potential of tidal current energy on its coast, and similar assessment surveys should be undertaken in the maritime provinces and Quebec.

In BC Hydro's 2002 'Tidal Current Energy' analysis completed by Triton Consultants, the following *advantages of Tidal energy* are listed in the Executive Summary:

- Tidal current energy is predictable—tides can be predicted centuries into the future

- Tidal current energy is regular—tidal currents follow a daily cycle

- Tidal current energy peaks at different times at different sites—power can be phased into the electricity grid.

- Tidal current energy will not be affected by global climate change

- Based on tidal modeling studies, environmental and physical impacts of tidal current power generation are expected to be small,

- *Tidal current resources in British Columbia are considerable*—the mean annual exploitable power ranges from about 2,700 GWh/annum for large scale installations with existing technology to approximately 20,000 GWh/annum with realistic assumptions on near future technology. *Note that 2,700 GWh and 20,000 GWh represent 5.6% and 40% respectively of BC Hydro's power generation in the year spanning 2001 to 2002.*

- Present tidal current energy generation costs, using currently demonstrated technology, appear to be competitive with other Green Energy sources, at 11¢/kWh for a large site (800 MW rated capacity and 1400 GWh/annum) and 25¢/kWh for a small site (43 MW rated capacity and 76 GWh/annum). These costs assume a conservative capacity factor (mean power/rated power) of 20% and a maximum current speed of 3.5 m/s.

- Future energy costs are expected to reduce considerably as both existing and new technologies are developed over the next few years. Assuming that maximum currents larger than 3.5 m/s can be exploited and present design developments continue, it is estimated that *future tidal current energy costs between 5¢/kWh and 7¢/kWh are achievable.*

3. In 2001 the Science and Technology Committee of the British Parliament released a comprehensive report, 'Tidal and Wave Energy' following an extensive inquiry. *The report recommends the British Government enhance opportunities to develop and deploy such systems and it identifies the following* benefits of ocean energy systems:

- Energy from both waves and tides is predictable and reliable, with few problems integrating the electricity into a modern Grid.

- Modern wave and tidal devices are based upon tried and tested engineering skills and experience, built up over fifty years of offshore oil and gas exploitation, in which the UK is particularly rich. There are already several prototypes working around the world—most notably on Islay in Western Scotland.

- Although more research needs to be carried out, the environmental impact of wave and tidal devices appears to be minimal. In fact, they can have a positive impact by stopping coastal erosion, for example.

- *The potential domestic and export market for wave and tidal energy devices is estimated to be worth between a half and one billion pounds. Were the UK to seize the lead now it could create a whole new industry employing thousands of people, as Denmark has already done with wind turbines.*

- The UK is particularly well placed to exploit both technologies, with a favourable wave climate and very strong tidal streams.

4. A 1994 report on Blue Energy Canada's Davis Hydro Turbine commissioned by the government of British Columbia stated, *"Many sites in B.C. and worldwide have the required conditions, deep, fast currents, to utilize the Davis turbine to produce commercial quantities of electricity."* . . . *"In suitable sites, and many seem to exist, significant quantities of electricity might be generated on scales comparable to conventional power plants (hydro, thermal, and nuclear)."* The report's author, Dr. Harold Halvorson (Halvorson Marine Engineers, Victoria) also said, "B.C. might benefit not only from using the technology to generate tidal electricity in the province but also from manufacturing units for domestic and export markets."

5. Large-scale tidal energy generation has been proposed for Passamaquoddy Bay straddling New Brunswick and Maine, and the Bay of Fundy since at least the 1930s. Even the late American President John F. Kennedy, a champion of a large-scale barrage-style tidal power project at 'Quoddy, envisioned a "fossil-fuel-free energy future" on the Atlantic seaboard. Newer tidal current technologies offer much more energy generation potential, and much less environmental disturbance, than the impoundment schemes advanced in earlier plans.

4

Tidal Power Is Too Costly to Replace Fossil Fuels

U.S. Department of Energy

The U.S. Department of Energy (DOE) advances the national, economic, and energy security of the United States. The DOE furthers energy technology and promotes energy innovation in the United States.

In parts of the world where tidal changes are significant, the currents created by the ebb and flow of tides can be converted into electricity. The technology to harness this power comes in three basic forms. Tidal barrages act as dams that force water through turbines that generate power. Tidal fences placed across channels use turnstile-like turbines to convert currents into power. Tidal turbines create power in the same way wind farms do, but they do so under water. Unfortunately, these tidal technologies impact the environment and are too costly to compete with the power produced by fossil fuels.

Some of the oldest ocean energy technologies use tidal power. All coastal areas consistently experience two high and two low tides over a period of slightly greater than 24 hours. For those tidal differences to be harnessed into electricity, the difference between high and low tides must be at least five meters, or more than 16 feet. There are only about 40 sites on the Earth with tidal ranges of this magnitude.

U.S. Department of Energy, "Ocean Tidal Power," December 30, 2008.

Currently, there are no tidal power plants in the United States. However, conditions are good for tidal power generation in both the Pacific Northwest and the Atlantic Northeast regions of the country.

The cost per kilowatt-hour of tidal power is not competitive with conventional fossil fuel power.

The Technologies

Tidal power technologies include the following:

Barrage or dam. A barrage or dam is typically used to convert tidal energy into electricity by forcing the water through turbines, activating a generator. Gates and turbines are installed along the dam. When the tides produce an adequate difference in the level of the water on opposite sides of the dam, the gates are opened. The water then flows through the turbines. The turbines turn an electric generator to produce electricity.

Tidal fence. Tidal fences look like giant turnstiles. They can reach across channels between small islands or across straits between the mainland and an island. The turnstiles spin via tidal currents typical of coastal waters. Some of these currents run at 5–8 knots (5.6–9 miles per hour) and generate as much energy as winds of much higher velocity. Because seawater has a much higher density than air, ocean currents carry significantly more energy than air currents (wind).

Tidal turbine. Tidal turbines look like wind turbines. They are arrayed underwater in rows, as in some wind farms. The turbines function best where coastal currents run at between 3.6 and 4.9 knots (4 and 5.5 mph). In currents of that speed, a 15-meter (49.2-feet) diameter tidal turbine can generate as much energy as a 60-meter (197-feet) diameter wind turbine. Ideal locations for tidal turbine farms are close to shore in water depths of 20–30 meters (65.5–98.5 feet).

Environmental and Economic Challenges

Tidal power plants that dam estuaries can impede sea life migration, and silt build-ups behind such facilities can impact local ecosystems. Tidal fences may also disturb sea life migration. Newly developed tidal turbines may prove ultimately to be the least environmentally damaging of the tidal power technologies because they don't block migratory paths.

It doesn't cost much to operate tidal power plants, but their construction costs are high and lengthen payback periods. As a result, the cost per kilowatt-hour of tidal power is not competitive with conventional fossil fuel power.

5

Wave Energy Is a Sound Alternative to Fossil Fuels

Enrique Gili

Enrique Gili, who lives, writes, and surfs in Ocean Beach, California, is a writer covering issues related to a healthy, sustainable lifestyle.

Engineers at Oregon State University are developing buoys that will convert the energy of waves into electricity. Not only is the constant rise and fall of waves a renewable power source, unlike fossil fuels, wave energy does not produce toxic greenhouse gases. Although the technology to convert waves into energy is still new and not yet commercially viable, wave energy ultimately could reduce U.S. dependence on fossil fuels. Moreover, wave energy projects could create jobs and bring money to the communities that take advantage of this new alternative energy source. Once developers address concerns about the impact on marine life, tourism, and recreation, wave power could take the lead as the nation's green power source.

Oregon's spectacular coastline could become the United States' center for wave energy development in coming years, with plans under way to install power buoys in locations with enough potential to meet the state's future energy needs.

Electrical engineers at Oregon State University are developing electricity-generating buoys they believe will be a key component for clean, green wave power. Their objective is to convert the Pacific Ocean's heavy rolling swell into a renewable energy resource, relying on buoys to harness the near constant rise and fall of waves to produce electricity.

"Waves generate energy through motion," said Dr. Annette von Jouanne, an electrical engineering professor at Oregon State University (OSU). The OSU project is part of a renewed global effort to investigate wave and tidal power as a potential source of alternative energy, she noted. "Oregon is an ideal location," von Jouanne added in an interview.

Along Oregon's 460 kilometers of open coastline, waves average 1.5 meters high during the summer months and 3.5 meters during the winter. To achieve their goals, von Jouanne and her colleagues at OSU have designed several types of power buoys, including oscillating linear generators they refer to as "direct drive" technology. "The devices directly convert the linear motion of the wave into electrical energy without any hydraulic or pneumatic stages," von Jouanne said.

Energy experts claim that harnessing just 0.2 percent of the ocean's untapped energy would meet the entire planet's power needs.

The upshot is a submersible buoy that can produce electricity without the risk of corrosive salt water wreaking havoc on its internal parts, and which is capable of withstanding the constant wear and tear of moving water that causes most machines to break down.

The buoy is composed of copper wire sheathed around a magnetic shaft made from high-density, rare earth materials, housed in a watertight chamber that forms an impermeable barrier. Tethered to the ocean floor with a heavy cable, the shaft remains fixed in place as the outer section bobs up and down in the water. That motion, coupled with a magnet moving through the center of a copper coil, generates electricity.

A Wave Energy Revival

Today, wave energy is undergoing a revival not seen since the OPEC [Organization of Petroleum Exporting Countries] energy crisis of the 1970s. At that time, ocean energy enjoyed a brief period of notoriety, as oil supplies slumped and the price of crude skyrocketed. However, interest waned as prices for fossil fuels dropped and incentives to develop alternative energy supplies evaporated. "Wave energy is still in its infancy," said Justin Klure, a senior energy advisor for Oregon State. "In order for ocean energy resources to be viable, advances need to be made in the technology and wave energy must be made affordable to consumers."

Nevertheless, Oregon is committed to developing renewable energy resources in order to cut overall greenhouse gas emissions and reduce the state's dependency on hydropower and fossil fuels. In the long term, 25 percent of Oregon's energy supply will come from wave, solar, and wind power, Klure said.

These efforts reflect renewed interest in the United States and elsewhere to use wave and tidal power to reduce fossil fuel dependency and to develop alternative sources of energy. Energy experts claim that harnessing just 0.2 percent of the ocean's untapped energy would meet the entire planet's power needs.

[As] the epicenter for a new industry focusing on wave technology . . . Oregon [will] become less dependent on fossil fuel and hydropower.

Testing Wave Power Feasibility

Currently several energy projects are under way to test the feasibility of wave power in Hawaii, Portugal and England. Klure compares wave power favourably to wind technology when that industry was in its earliest stages of development 15 years ago [in about 1992]. When specialists began advocating the use of wind power for large-scale energy projects, modern-day wind farms were a promising though untested technology. Initially, wind turbines were expensive to produce and unwieldy. Over time, their fabrication, design and efficiency improved dramatically.

With the development of von Jouanne's prototypes and plans for a wave farm near Gardiner, Oregon hopes to become the epicenter for a new industry focusing on wave technology. Not only will Oregon become less dependent on fossil fuel and hydropower, but in the process become the "Boeing" corporation of wave energy technology, bringing investment and jobs to the region, said Klure.

Western Oregon's paucity of sunshine also makes wave technology appealing to state regulators. Water is 800 more times dense than air so the amount of energy extractable from ocean power is exponentially that much greater. Also, when compared to wind and solar power, waves are more consistent. Incoming swell can be predicted with 80 percent accuracy and is virtually constant. A buoy measuring three meters high, bobbing up and down in the ocean, could produce 250 kilowatts per unit—meaning a modest-sized network of about 200 buoys could illuminate the downtown business district of Portland [Oregon].

Theoretically, a grid of wave farms established along Oregon's shoreline could produce most if not all of the state's energy needs. However, the state's renewable energy objectives are far more modest, with an overall goal to produce 500 megawatts of wave power within 20 years, and plans for wave power remain just that. Before wave farms are fully implemented, renewable energy has to be balanced with concerns over the impact on marine resources and the effect on tourism and the recreation industry.

Power buoys could pose their own unforeseen threat to wildlife. If those concerns are dealt with, Oregon's clean green wave power could lead the nation in developing renewable energy resources.

6

The Environmental Impact of Wave Energy Remains Unknown

Michelle Ma

Michelle Ma is a staff reporter for the Seattle Times.

The rush to convert energy from ocean waves to electricity has slowed, primarily due to concerns about the environmental impacts of wave energy devices. For example, wave energy buoys could alter ecosystems or disrupt whale and fish migration. The fishing industry fears that wave and tidal projects could further reduce access to fishing grounds. Still others fear that without adequate study beforehand, the use of such devices could change the character of U.S. coasts. Despite these concerns, however, in the Pacific Northwest, researchers from the University of Washington and Oregon State University are studying the cost effectiveness and environmental suitability of potential sites for the production of wave and tidal energy.

What started out as a mad dash to extract energy from the ocean's waves and tides has slowed to a marathoner's pace—complete with a few water breaks and sprained ankles along the way.

In the past three years [since 2005], more than 100 preliminary permits have been issued nationally for wave- and tidal-energy projects, and nearly 100 more are pending approval. But only one has won a license to operate—a small wave-energy development off Washington's northwest coast.

That project is still awaiting state and federal permits, and its British Columbia–based developer, Finavera Renewables, doesn't know when the first devices will go in the water. It doesn't help that a wave-power buoy the company was testing off the Oregon coast unexpectedly sank [in November 2007].

No one knows exactly how the technologies will behave in the water, whether animals will get hurt, or if costs will pencil out.

An Unknown Technology

Tapping the power of waves and tidal currents to generate electricity is promoted as one of many promising alternatives to the fossil fuels that contribute to global warming.

But no one knows exactly how the technologies will behave in the water, whether animals will get hurt, or if costs will pencil out. The permitting process is expensive and cumbersome, and no set method exists for getting projects up and running.

"The industry is really young, and everything is hodgepodged right now," said Jim Thomson, an oceanographer at the University of Washington's Applied Physics Lab who is involved in tidal research.

A new report that collected findings from dozens of scientists raises concerns about the impact wave-energy developments could have on the ocean and its critters. Wave-energy buoys could alter the food chain or disrupt migrations, the report says.

Still, developers, regulators and researchers are moving forward. A 2.25-megawatt project off the coast of Portugal went on line [in fall 2008], becoming the world's first commercial wave-energy development in operation. It can supply 1,500 households with electricity.

The first commercial wave-energy park in the U.S. could go in off Reedsport, Ore., within the next two years.

Tidal energy has yet to go commercial, but devices have been tested in Ireland and Canada. Turbines have been placed in New York's East River, and a demonstration project is planned for the Bay of Fundy off the Northeastern U.S.

In the Northwest, the Snohomish County [Washington] Public Utility District (PUD) has narrowed its search for tidal-power sites in Puget Sound, although the PUD doesn't expect to have a test project in the water for another two years.

The Race to Develop

Dozens of developers have staked claim to plots in the ocean and in waterways that could provide wave and tidal energy. But despite the jostle for space, getting projects off dry land has proved difficult.

Wave-power generators use the up-and-down motion of the ocean's swells to produce electricity. Tidal generators act like underwater windmills, spinning as the tides move in and out.

To get small projects in the water quicker federal regulators recently created a five-year pilot license for tidal and wave developments. That's meant to help developers gather data they need to launch future projects, said Federal Energy Regulatory Commission spokeswoman Celeste Miller.

Yet even with a more streamlined process, no one has applied for the pilot license, Miller said. Finavera received its license for the 1-megawatt Makah Bay [Washington] wave project before this option became available.

Given the unknowns in a young industry, it's not surprising projects are taking longer than some developers would like, said Myke Clark, senior vice president of business development for Finavera.

His company encountered another hurdle when Pacific Gas and Electric's agreement to buy power from a planned Finavera wave-energy project off California was rejected [in October 2008] by the state's Public Utilities Commission.

Regulators said the rates were too high and the buoy technology not yet ready.

Clark said the decision wouldn't affect Finavera's Makah Bay project.

The environmental effects of wave and tidal energy are largely unknown and require more studies.

Research Is Under Way

Researchers from the University of Washington [UW] and Oregon State University [OSU] hope that a new national marine renewable-energy research center in the Northwest will help answer questions about tidal and wave energy.

A federal grant provides $1.25 million annually for up to five years. The UW will continue research on tidal energy in Puget Sound, while OSU will focus on wave energy.

"The feeling is that a lot of questions being asked now are only questions that can be answered with a responsible pilot [project]," said Brian Polagye, who is pursuing his doctorate in mechanical engineering at the UW.

Locally, researchers want to see where marine life in Puget Sound congregates and to create a standard way to evaluate sites around the country to determine which would be good candidates for tidal-energy projects.

Admiralty Inlet, between Whidbey Island and Port Townsend, is the likely spot for the Snohomish County PUD's small test project set to launch at least two years from now [in 2010–11], said Craig Collar, the PUD's senior manager of energy-resource development.

The inlet's tides are strong, and the area is large enough to accommodate a tidal project without interfering with other activities such as diving and ferry traffic.

Finavera wants to install four wave-energy buoys in Makah Bay in the Olympic Coast National Marine Sanctuary to test its technology. Developers also plan to monitor the project for effects on wildlife and shoreline habitat, keeping an eye on federally listed species such as the marbled murrelet, a small bird that dives for food.

Finavera doesn't intend to continue the project after its five-year license expires. Still, if the company can negotiate a purchasing agreement with the Clallam County Public Utility District, homes in the area could use the wave-generated power while the project is in the water, Clark said.

The Makah Nation wants to see what effect the project might have on the environment before deciding whether wave energy is a viable long-term option, said Ryland Bowechop, tourism and economic-development planner for the tribe.

The buoys would sit just offshore from the tribal headquarters in Neah Bay.

"We are always concerned because our livelihood is the ocean," Bowechop said.

Fishermen have their own worries. They fear that wave and tidal projects could further reduce access to fishing grounds.

Concerns Linger

The environmental effects of wave and tidal energy are largely unknown and require more studies, dozens of scientists concluded after meeting a year ago at OSU's Hatfield Marine Science Center in Newport, Ore.

The group was concerned that electromagnetic cables on the ocean floor could affect sea life, and that buoys could interfere with whale and fish migration.

Large buoys might actually attract more fish, but the marine ecosystem could be altered if more predators move in. Buoys also could disrupt natural currents and change how sediment is moved. Shorelines might be affected as energy is taken from the waves.

Even if environmental concerns are checked, costs to extract the power remain high. Wave energy costs at least 20 cents per kilowatt hour to generate, compared with 4 cents per kilowatt hour for wind power, said Annette von Jouanne, leader of OSU's wave-energy program. Wind energy used to be much more expensive 20 years ago.

In comparison, coal-generated power costs about 5 cents per kilowatt hour, and power from dams can be as low as 3 cents, said Roger Bedard, ocean-energy leader with the nonprofit Electric Power Research Institute.

Tidal-energy costs are harder to determine because there aren't any projects trying to sell electricity, Bedard said.

Fishermen have their own worries. They fear that wave and tidal projects could further reduce access to fishing grounds, said Dale Beasley, a commercial fisherman in Ilwaco, Pacific County, and president of the Columbia River Crab Fisherman's Association.

"There's so many things coming at the ocean right now," he said.

Beasley says the industry wants a say in how wave- and tidal-energy projects are developed.

"Coastal communities are going to have to figure out a way to deal with this, and if they don't, the character of the coast will change dramatically," he said.

7

Tidal Energy Companies Should Expect Reasoned Environmental Opposition

Ed Friedman and Kathleen McGee

Ed Friedman is chairman of Friends of Merrymeeting Bay, an organization whose goal is to preserve, protect, and improve the unique ecosystems of Merrymeeting Bay, Maine. Kathleen McGee is a social justice activist working in Maine.

When tidal energy companies seek permits without considering the environmental impact of their projects, they should not blame local organizations for choosing to withdraw from these projects. Some fledgling tidal energy companies without well-planned alternative energy projects seek preliminary permits with the goal of grabbing land. Local environmental advocates simply seek evidence that the projects pose no threat to sensitive environmental areas. Often it is the failure of tidal power companies to keep their promise to communicate with stakeholders during the planning process that leads to project failure, not the reasoned objections of local environmental advocates.

As a parting corporate shot [in June 2009], Oceana Energy cited, twice, "local hostility" as the reason it would not pursue a tidal energy project at The Chops [a rock formation in the mouth of Maine's Kennebec River] in Merrymeeting Bay.

The public has been inundated with this disingenuous rhetoric from big corporate biz: too much regulation or "local

Ed Friedman and Kathleen McGee, "The Chops: The Wrong Location for a Tidal Energy Project," *Brunswick (ME) Times Record*, June 12, 2009. Reproduced by permission of the authors. www.friendsofmerrymeetingbay.org.

hostility" made them leave, not their own greed or poor management. The corporate mantra, unfortunately, is as effective as it is old and worn out.

The truth of the Oceana matter lies in its own printed decision: "(Oceana) has conducted a review of the environmental sensitivity of the Kennebec River area site . . . and determined that insufficient development potential exists for pursuit of either a full development or pilot project there."

Further, Oceana did not deliver on its promise to work with state, federal and local agencies as well as environmental groups as it developed the tidal energy project at The Chops.

Flagrantly misleading in its required six-month filing, Oceana stated: "METidal and its environmental permitting consultants have had continuing discussions about this project with various stakeholders, including resource agencies, environmental advocacy groups, and prospective project partners. . . .

"METidal will continue to engage regulatory agencies, state and federal resource agencies, tribal entities, environmental groups, academic institutions and the public to identify and understand possibilities for resolution of potential multi-use conflicts, as well as environmental issues and concerns. . . ."

A Failure to Engage

There is little or no evidence that METidal did anything of the kind. They certainly did not talk to any relevant environmental groups (Friends of Merrymeeting Bay, Chewonki, Conservation Law Foundation) in the Merrymeeting Bay area.

Friends of Merrymeeting Bay is a local environmental organization. Our mission: To preserve, protect, and improve the unique ecosystems of Merrymeeting Bay. To that end we also work statewide on issues ranging from appropriate siting for alternative energy, land conservation, fish restoration through improved fish passage at dams, toxic use reduction, etc., as well as education and advocacy to achieve our long-term vision that includes balance with environmental and economic concerns.

About two years ago [in 2007] there was a tidal wave, pun intended, of permits that hit the state for tidal energy projects. Some speculated it was no more than multiple land grabs. Even the Federal Energy Regulatory Commission acknowledged the issue of and potential problems with "site banking" via the widespread acquisition of "preliminary permits."

Oceana Energy requested a permit for underwater turbines at the 280-yard opening at The Chops in Merrymeeting Bay. Little information was available for the extent of the project, except to say there could be up to 50 turbines each 20 feet to 50 feet wide, not unlike wind turbines we've become acquainted with, stretched across the small opening that drains the six rivers that comprise Merrymeeting Bay.

Up to 50 turbines: A 280-yard wide opening.

Honest concerns don't make [local environmental advocates] hostile, just credible.

A Reasoned Intervention

Friends of Merrymeeting Bay intervened in order to be informed and also state our objections to placing one of these yet-to-be determined projects in a highly environmentally sensitive area without more scrutiny.

We just finished a long-term current study of the Bay. One might assume the water rushing down from six rivers would wash through to the ocean once it cleared the narrows at The Chops. But our study showed it is actually much the same water flowing back and forth through that very narrow opening constantly every day.

And back and forth with the current also go the sturgeon, salmon, alewives, seals, striped bass, eels, etc., not to mention, navigationally, the jet skis, power boats, ice breakers, sailboats, kayakers, canoeists and even four-foot pulp wood from years ago. An already ailing fishery would be subjected to numerous exposures to turbines hour after hour, day after day, week after week. Navigation also becomes a concern in an already turbulent section of river. Cumulative impact becomes a huge factor.

Alternative energy is critical to both our environmental and economic health. In the world's haste, partially to reduce CO_2 [carbon dioxide] emissions, partly to jump onto the latest moneymaker and partly to appear "Green" (greenwash), we have skipped some steps of wisdom in the "who, what, where, when" scenario.

While we may be running short of time to turn this environmental Titanic around, we surely have even less time for unintended consequences.

Friends of Merrymeeting Bay rationally debated the pros and cons of a tidal project at The Chops. Because we work statewide on issues we hardly consider our approach "NIMBY" (used mostly but often without merit pejoratively, a term meaning "not in my back yard"). We believe there are many good places wide and deep enough along the Kennebec, and other rivers and bays that could host a pilot project.

The Chops, as a chokepoint for the entire 10,000 square mile watershed, is not one of them.

Due Diligence

Friends of Merrymeeting Bay did due diligence in our opposition to the tidal project at The Chops. There is little question we played a role in the decision to withdraw the permit and it is our hope it will not be a site in the future. Our determination was based on the bay being high value habitat for all 12 diadromous [migrating from freshwater to seawater] fish species of the Gulf of Maine and The Chops providing the only (and limited) access.

Our belief that we need to protect those nursery habitats and spawning grounds in order to revive our dying native fishing industry is both environmentally and economically based and we see great merit and wisdom in preventing a bad project planned for the wrong location.

Friends of Merrymeeting Bay is pleased that METidal chose to forego the Chops project. We believe this benefits us both environmentally and economically. We are disappointed it chose to take a parting shot at our community by saying it was "local hostility" that determined its choice.

Evidence available shows we were resolute but well reasoned. We are not "local hostiles" but local advocates, a voice for the few places left natural, not despoiled for the sake of "progress." Oceana is making excuses for a bad idea gone south. We didn't bully them out of the area or harass them; we presented facts backed by pertinent research to reflect our position.

Our honest concerns don't make us hostile, just credible.

8

Wave Turbines Pose a Threat to Marine Mammals

Mark Macaskill

Mark Macaskill is a senior writer for the Sunday Times, *the Sunday edition of the* Times *of London.*

Marine biologists warn that wave power turbines may pose a threat to marine mammals. Marine mammal sonar may be inadequate to detect the sixteen-meter-wide blades of the turbines in time to avoid injury. These biologists also fear that fish seeking shelter near the turbines will attract whales, which might then be killed by the turbines. The Scottish Association for Marine Science (SAMS) fears that not enough is known about marine mammal behavior around the turbines and suggests further study. SAMS is not opposed to renewable energy but recommends caution until the impact on marine mammals is clearer.

Plans to build the world's biggest wave farm off the Scottish coast could have a devastating impact on whales, dolphins and seals, scientists have warned.

Marine biologists fear the mammals, which have poor eyesight, will be unable to detect the underwater turbines in time using sonar and will be injured or killed by the rotating 16m-wide blades.

Scientists also fear that fish may shelter around or below the turbines, luring larger predators such as whales to their deaths.

The warning, published in a report by the Scottish Association for Marine Science (SAMS) follows plans to harness the power of the ocean and produce green energy by installing hundreds of turbines, on the seabed in the Pentland Firth, between the Scottish mainland and Orkney [an archipelago in northern Scotland].

Ministers [of state] believe it could transform the area into the "Saudi Arabia of marine energy".

However, marine biologists warn sea mammals may have less than a second's warning to reverse course and avoid a fatal collision. Research has shown that larger mammals typically take more than a second to perform a U-turn.

Not enough is known about the environmental impacts of marine renewable energy devices on sea creatures.

Many Unknowns

The study by SAMS concludes that not enough is known about the environmental impacts of marine renewable energy devices on sea creatures and that more time is needed to assess the risks.

"Depending upon the conditions, tidal devices may not be acoustically detectable in time for marine mammals to avoid collision," the study states. "Under these circumstances it is probable that there would not be enough time for an animal to avoid the device. A further consideration is that, with this magnitude of warning time, the animal is likely to be very close to the device. Since these devices are large, the closer the marine mammals are, the greater their avoidance manoeuvre will need to be."

The study suggests possible solutions might be to fit the turbines with "pingers", which emit bursts of sound to deter animals, to install protective netting to prevent collisions, or to put warning lights on blades, but it acknowledges there is no guarantee these measures could prevent mammals colliding with the devices.

Another measure, they suggest, would be to switch off the turbines during the breeding season, although this would mean less energy being produced.

More than three dozen energy companies are hoping to install turbines in the Pentland Firth after the Crown Estate announced plans [in 2008] to lease the seabed to developers.

The channel of water contains six of the top 10 sites in the UK [United Kingdom] for tidal energy. It is hoped its power could be harnessed to generate 700MW [megawatts] of electricity by 2020, enough for about 400,000 homes.

"We are trying to understand how seals and dolphins will behave around these devices," said Dr Ben Wilson, marine ecologist at SAMS, who supervised the study. "I don't think people realise how imminent it is that turbines will be a feature of the Scottish marine environment. We are not against renewable energy but it needs to be done right.

"Agile marine mammals collide with man-made objects; it's not uncommon. They will not expect to find these devices in the water and the last thing we want is to backtrack after finding out that there is a problem."

Ship strikes are a known cause of mortality for both whales and dolphins worldwide. Although precise numbers are not known, it is thought such collisions account for up to 47% of recovered carcases.

9

Active Sonar May Help Monitor the Impact on Marine Mammals

Lesley Riddoch

Lesley Riddoch is a Scottish broadcaster, journalist, and commentator who runs an independent radio and podcast company from Abertay University in Dundee, Scotland. She also is a weekly columnist for the Scotsman, *a Scottish daily newspaper.*

Monitoring marine mammals to determine whether tidal power turbines pose a serious threat is costly. At present, operators of turbines look for marine life from the turbine bridge or by using sonar at the stern of turbines. If such observers spot a seal, they turn off the turbines. Unfortunately, distinguishing seals from seaweed and other objects can be difficult, and sometimes the turbines are needlessly shut down. Launching the fledgling tidal power industry will be difficult until less costly monitoring methods can be found. Active sonar may be the answer. Once active sonar is trained to differentiate seals from other objects, it may reveal what seals actually do near turbines. If seals recognize the danger and swim away, tidal turbine power can then proceed without costly monitoring.

Active sonar is being 'trained' to identify sea mammals in a bid to cut the costs of monitoring tidal turbines and speed up the development of marine energy in Britain. The sonar is just one part of the technological response to a very

Lesley Riddoch, "Listening In: Comms Active Sonar: Could Active Sonar Systems Trained by Humans, Help Unlock Tidal Energy in the UK?" *Engineering & Technology*, vol. 4, August 08–September 11, 2009. Reproduced by permission.

human—and animal—problem. Will underwater turbines harm seals, dolphins and seabirds? And how would we know if they did?

The world's largest environmental marine-energy monitoring project in Northern Ireland has not found that tidal turbines are having a measurable impact on seals, dolphins and seabirds after three years of a five-year study. But, while marine biologists say it could take a decade to be sure, developers say more expensive monitoring could cripple the fledgling tidal energy industry. Academics are hoping technology might offer a compromise.

Costly Marine Mammal Monitoring

Bristol-based tidal energy developer Marine Current Turbines (MCT) has already spent £3m [3 million pounds Sterling] on detailed monitoring work around its twin-turbine SeaGen device, installed [in 2008] in Strangford Lough near Belfast.

The monitoring work was agreed with the Northern Ireland Environment Agency to ameliorate the impact of locating turbines in a national nature reserve with nine EU [European Union] habitat and wildlife designations and an established seal colony, and it is largely visual in its method. A marine mammal observer stands on SeaGen's bridge, ready to hit an 'off' button if a seal appears within 50m [50 meters]. A colleague sits in the stern using sonar to spot seals underwater, although it's hard to distinguish the sonar signals created by a seal pup from those created by a clump of seaweed.

Meanwhile, experts from the St Andrews–based Sea Mammal Research Unit (SMRU) have attached transmitters to the hair on seals' heads to help track their movements. The devices—which use mobile phone technology—come off when the animals moult.

Finally, biologist Daryl Birkett has conducted eight surveys a month for the past three years from a grassy knoll opposite

SeaGen, using range-finding binoculars to note every sea mammal, seabird, or human movement in the Narrows.

Queens University marine biologist Graham Savidge says the half million movements recorded so far suggest turbines and seals avoid one another:

"Few seals are found in the fast currents that turbines need—on the surface at least. The majority prefer the lower water speeds of the lough's margins."

The sonar's primary use is to see what animals actually do near turbines. It's quite possible seals may be attracted, get close and then swim safely away.

Conflicting Reports

Martin Wright, managing director of MCT is "profoundly pleased and relieved" the turbines have not had any measurable impact on Strangford wildlife, but says the cost of proving that has been onerous.

"There will be no further tidal projects with this level of monitoring. Tidal energy will not happen if an embryonic industry is made to carry such burdens. . . ."

Professor Ian Boyd of SMRU disagrees: "The effect of turbines on sea mammals will only become apparent over a period of ten years. We know that porpoises, for example, are already spending less time in the Strangford narrows and there may be other effects that are not measurable using current methods. So monitoring must continue—at test sites and at sea. The marine [energy] industry is not viable unless it can carry these costs."

No seal appears to have been injured by the turbines, fishing boats, yachts or the Portaferry-Strangford ferry, which makes 64 crossings per day.

But common seal numbers around Britain are 30–40 per cent down in a decade, so just one turbine-related death would be serious for tidal developers, because EU rules ban developments that pose new threats to endangered species.

Active Sonar Tracks

St Andrews–based SMRU believes the solution could be the development of active sonar, as [it] is already used to find undersea objects such as pipelines, in naval tracking and in ultrasound for expectant mothers. But none of the sonar kits currently in use offer all the features needed to monitor a tidal turbine. So SMRU and the Orkney-based European Marine Energy Centre (EMEC) are 'training' DT-X sonar technology from Seattle-based BioSonics, using 'spotter' sightings to corroborate and improve recognition.

This summer [2009] marine biologists will collect data on the swimming and diving behaviour of marine mammals. This will provide the basis for Biosonics' engineering staff to program their classification software to differentiate between swimming animals and other targets such as seaweed or submerged logs. They will use 'detection matrices'—software processes that try to classify moving blobs on a sonar screen into categories such as 'marine mammal', 'debris', or 'seabird', based on factors such as its acoustic target strength, size, swimming speed and diving behaviour. It's hoped that this will allow the sonar to automatically detect and track animals in 3D around tidal turbines.

But Wright at turbine company MCT questions the utility of 'seal sonar'.

"Seals are high-order predators adapted to their environment, a bit like taxis in central London, which come within inches of passers-by but there are no body bags at the end of the day. Seals appear to understand the tidal turbines and if there is no measurable impact then no further mitigation—human monitoring or sonar—should be needed."

Jenny Norris from EMEC believes seal sonar will be helpful to those who believe seals aren't at risk from turbines at all.

"The sonar's primary use is to see what animals actually do near turbines. It's quite possible seals may be attracted, get close and then swim safely away, without any physical interaction," she says. "If devices are always shut down when animals are sighted, we will never know what seals do next. The sonar will help us find out and that's why it will probably trigger an alarm—not go for automatic shutdown."

An EU marine research project could help settle the issue. Equimar involves 61 scientists, developers, engineers and conservationists from 11 European countries finding ways to measure and compare tidal- and wave-energy devices so governments can back the best models.

If [tidal power] devices are always shut down when animals are sighted, we will never know what seals do next. The sonar will help us find out.

According to its Edinburgh-based coordinator, Dr David Ingram: "Early devices need extensive tests and test sites should be as highly instrumented as possible. But if tests demonstrate turbines have no measurable impact on sea mammals, then the monitoring and observation burden for future projects has to be much lower. If 'seal sonar' works, our protocols could require its use in test sites—sonar wouldn't then be needed for successfully tested devices at sea."

Wright may take some convincing: "Computers are not good at pattern recognition—I fear that if sonar is made compulsory for tidal turbines at sea it will cause shutdowns all the time. No human surveillance will be possible there. So monitoring will cause chaos when we deploy arrays of turbines to generate substantial tidal energy."

Professor Boyd concedes active sonar is sensitive to air bubbles in the water column and doesn't currently work as well near the surface. But since tidal devices are underwater, sonar is most accurate where seals might be in most danger of collision.

"I hope by next year, accurate sonar at £15,000 per turbine will be on the market ... for marine developers that isn't going to break the bank."

10

Wave Energy Projects Should Consider the Views of the Surfing Community

Peter M. Connor

Peter M. Connor is a renewable energy policy professor at the University of Exeter in Cornwall, England.

When seeking approval for wave energy projects such as the proposed Wave Hub off the coast of Cornwall, England, developers should include all stakeholders, including members of the surfing community, in the process. The wave energy potential that attracts those who hope to turn wave power into electricity is also what attracts surfers. Unfortunately, the results of studies about the impact of wave energy technology vary, and their interpretation by the media has in some cases been misleading. While some high-profile surfers oppose the Wave Hub, most surfers generally support environmental concerns. Indeed, many surfers support wave power projects as a renewable energy resource. Thus, to gain surfers' trust, developers should consult with them during the approval process and should share the best available research regarding the impacts of the use of such technology.

Wave Hub is a sub-sea electrical grid connection point proposed for installation on the seabed 15–20km [kilometers] off the north coast of Cornwall, in the southwest of the UK [United Kingdom].

If planning approval is granted then the Wave Hub will provide a direct connection to the UK distribution network. It will be initially capable of transmitting up to 20MW [mega-watts] of power, with the potential to be upgraded to 40MW if demand is sufficient. The site is intended to allow demonstration phase wave energy generating devices to connect to the grid, thus allowing direct sales of any electricity generated. Local government support from the SW Regional Development Agency (SWRDA) effectively acts to assume some of the risk of capital investment in grid connection in exchange for site rental, whilst also allowing sales of electricity and Renewables Obligation Certificates. SWRDA is also hopeful that the location of the Wave Hub, combined with other initiatives may act to attract new industry to the SW peninsula.

As well as attempting to push forward the commercialisation of wave energy technology, the site will see the operation of multiple arrays of wave energy devices in a relatively small area, only 1km x 3km (with an additional 500m [meter] exclusion boundary, for a total area of 2km x 4km). This close proximity of devices is unusual in devices already installed around the world, allowing data to be collected as to how this impacts on overall performance of multiple device types.

The Hub thus offers potential for stimulating new research, for opportunities to advance the operational characteristics of wave energy technology and for capture of socioeconomic benefits to the investing region. . . .

[One] source of [wave] resource conflict . . . stems from the surf sector.

Competing for Wave Resources

Whilst it is possible to identify multiple potential benefits of the development of the Wave Hub to the southwest region of the UK, including local economic and social benefits, as well as wider environmental and technological gains, the Cornish coast, as with the rest of the UK are already subject to a wide range of uses. There are two main areas of resource conflict arising from the siting of the Wave Hub. Firstly, the fishing industry is a significant source of employment in Cornwall and reductions in available area for exploitation are potentially controversial. The relatively small size of the area which will be off limits to shipping, including the fishing fleet, as a result of the Wave has not so far led to any notable controversy.

The second source of resource conflict . . . stems from the surf sector. Surfing has grown to be a major leisure activity in the southwest of England, with Cornwall being the location of many of the UK's leading surf beaches. Surfing has been estimated to bring a direct spend of £21 million (€31 million) annually to the county. Surfing in the UK, with very limited exceptions, relies on the delivery of wave energy at the shoreline with surfers utilising waves up to a maximum of a few hundred metres from the shore. Given the direction of the swells at the Wave Hub location any wave energy devices installed at the Wave Hub will draw power from waves which are incident on the section of the north Cornish coast. This stretch of coastline is approximately 35km long and includes a number of popular surf beaches including the town of Newquay, a tourist town which relies for much of its popularity on surfing.

It is the uncertainty over [wave impact] figures that is the source of conflict with regard to the Wave Hub [wave energy project] and the surf community.

Since wave energy is proportional to the square of wave height, it is readily apparent that exploitation of wave energy for electrical generation will act to deplete the waves immediately beyond a wave energy device. What is not certain is how far this effect will extend beyond the device—or array of devices—and what will be the extent of the effect over distance from the devices. It is the uncertainty over these figures that is the source of conflict with regard to the Wave Hub and the surf community.

The Impacts on Shoreline Wave Height

Two published attempts—the first by the South West Regional Development Agency, the second by [D.L. Millar, H.C.M. Smith, and D.E. Reeve (2007)]—have tried to model the impacts of the Wave Hub on shoreline wave climate, neither of which can be regarded as being definitive. The reports take a different approach to modelling and problems can be identified with each. The first of the two to be published was a report carried out on behalf of the South West Regional Development Agency, by the consultancy group Halcrow, as part of its assessment of the Wave Hub and the range of potential impacts. It concluded that there would be a measurable impact on shoreline wave climate along the section of Cornish coast from St Ives Bay to Harlyn Bay, with variations in the level of impact over the range of locations, and with different sea conditions. . . .

The second published set of models was produced by Millar et al., and despite a publication date in 2007 became publicly available around September 2006. Employing a potentially more complex model, though with different input criteria, the results of this work suggested somewhat lesser impacts than those produced by the Halcrow model. Millar et al. employ data to more closely reflect actual wave behaviour off Cornwall rather than the idealised 'surfer's wave' situation. Thus they attempt to take into account both swell and wind waves. Shoreline effects of energy device installation at the Wave Hub are modelled for multiple values of energy absorption. . . .

It is clear that there is a need for further work to be carried out to understand the impacts operational wave energy devices have on local wave climate. This is necessary both generally and in the specific instance of the Wave Hub. Prior to that however, then decisions must either be deferred or made based on the available information.

Interpretation by the Press

Despite the relatively small number of models and the relatively low levels of impact they predict on the shoreline wave climate, there have been a much wider range of figures propagated in the public domain. Some of these seem to have come from the published reports, albeit often stripped of context, while others have no readily identifiable source.

The publication by Halcrow of data concerning potential shoreline impacts stemming from the Wave Hub was picked up by some elements of the UK national and regional press. A *Sunday Times* article in July 2006 was one of the first to mention the potential shoreline effects of the Wave Hub, it began with the statement 'The £20m [million] offshore chain of pumps and turbines will affect a 20-mile stretch of beaches, reducing the height of the waves by more than 10%', but made no further attempt to add any clarification as to the context in which these circumstances might occur. The figure appears to have been taken from the Halcrow report, though there it is made clear that it will occur only in rare conditions. The remainder of the article is primarily concerned with outlining the economic and social implications of the stated drop in wave height, and of the conflict between the Cornish surf economy and community on one side and the Wave Hub developers on the other.

The *Sunday Times* article was picked up by the regional press and other news outlets. Regional newspapers including the West Briton and the *Western Morning News* ran articles in the days following the *Sunday Times* article that appeared to be based largely around the information made available in the *Sunday Times*, with the 11% reduction in wave height at the shoreline being repeated. The BBC's news website commented on the conflict, quoting a representative of the pro-Wave Hub Surfers Against Sewage as saying the effect of the Wave Hub on shoreline wave climate "would be an 11% reduction in surf height at most", this qualification of the 11% figure was relatively uncommon. The same figure, again without any of the situation-specific context of the Halcrow report, reached the Scottish national press in 2007 via [news service] Reuters.

From July 2006 onwards, the issue of Wave Hub impacts on shoreline wave climate and potential implications for surfers began to attract more attention in the surf community, though it is certainly possible that it was members of the surf community opposed to the Wave Hub who had brought the attention of the national and regional press to the issue in July 2006.

Vocal Opponents

One of the most vocal opponents of the Wave Hub based on its perceived potential impacts on shoreline waves has been John Baxendale. Baxendale, a surf enthusiast and current member of the executive board of the British Surfing Association (BSA) operates a surf forecasting company in Cornwall. Baxendale formerly acted as webmaster for the website 'A1 surf', popular amongst the surf community for weather and surf reports and for surf related news. Baxendale initiated a petition on the A1 surf site which attracted 600+ signatures asking for further consultation with surfers before Wave Hub construction be initiated. This petition was submitted to the Department of Trade and Industry [DTI]—the government department responsible for supporting efforts in wave energy—as part of a review initiated by the DTI to investigate Wave hub impacts.

Other representatives of the BSA also appear to oppose the Wave Hub. A statement purporting to represent the position of the BSA was produced on August 8th 2006 by Ben Farwagi, a member of the Executive Board of the BSA. The statement employs the outlying 13% figure likely to come from the Halcrow report. However, Farwagi makes two further propositions, firstly that the Wave Hub could have a potential 30% reduction on wave height at the shoreline, and implicitly that this might apply in all conditions with commensurate negative implications for surf quality. The 30% figure appears to be pure hypothesis on behalf of Farwagi and the BSA, and the assumption does not attempt to take into account the variation in impacts dependent on wave height assumed by modellers. The BSA, claiming 10,000 members, is the closest thing to a national body representing the interests of surfers in the UK. If it is able to leverage its access to these surfers then it has the potential to use them to support its policy positions.

Following a further report from Black in 2007 which suggested similar results to Halcrow, though with the potential for greater reductions in wave height in some—relatively rare—conditions, the Environment Committee of the BSA released a statement accepting the installation of the Wave Hub provided that it was monitored for effect as recommended within Black's report and on the basis that future developments would also be subject to stakeholder consultation.

The Position of the Surf Community

While there appears to have been assumptions on the part of much of the press that surfers are against the development of the Wave hub, this is not necessarily the case. The position of the surf community in Cornwall with regard to the Wave Hub is not homogeneous. The national surf body, the British Surf Association (BSA) appears to oppose the Wave Hub or at least has been represented as such by its officers. The environmentally leaning Surfers Against Sewage (SAS) supports the development of the Wave Hub and wave energy generally. The division also extends to the UK surf press, with *Carve* magazine taking an editorial perspective opposing the Wave Hub, while

Drift magazine has broadly supported it and the editor of *Surfer's Path* magazine has gone on record with concerns that opposition to the Wave Hub will damage the reputation of surfers with regard to environmental concern.

The [Wave Hub power project] issue could almost be designed for creating division in the surf community.

The issue could almost be designed for creating division in the surf community. Surfing in the UK and elsewhere has a history of pro-environmental activity. The NGO [nongovernmental organization] Surfers Against Sewage (SAS) have taken a very active role in campaigning for improved water quality around the UK coast over the last two decades, as well as actively addressing other environmental issues. SAS have issued a number of statements in support of the Wave Hub, emphasising the issue of global warming and emissions relating to fossil fuel energy use. They have taken particular care to emphasise the particular published results relating to shoreline wave modelling. The SAS position can be regarded as reflecting a worldview amongst many surfers that is generally protective of the environment. The Wave Hub, however, offers a potential conflict between this perspective and a perceived threat to the basic resource necessary for surfers. This conflict is at the heart of the divide over the Wave Hub issue.

If surfers are to be a key stakeholder group impacting on the approval process of the Wave Hub then it is important that as a group they are basing their position on the best available information. The balance of opinion is likely to correlate with both the quality of information available but also with the access to information that members of the stakeholder community have. This increases the importance of both producing accurate information and of ensuring its wider dissemination.

The Implications for Wave Energy

Some degree of conflict over resources that might be useful to renewable energy generation as well as to other uses may be inevitable. It may be possible to resolve conflict with good will, however, the nature of conflict between different parties within society, the ways in which opinions are formed, means to produce the most optimal outputs that the positions that are taken by the various stakeholders must be rooted in information that is as accurate as possible. This is true from both perspectives in the case of wave energy. Models which predict impacts markedly less than actually occur may result in decisions with more significant ecological and social impacts than would otherwise have been acceptable, perhaps sufficient to have disallowed installation if presented prior to approval. Equally, information—or misinformation—exaggerating the impacts of wave energy devices or arrays could attract greater opposition to proposed installations. . . .

There is a need for wave energy developers . . . to be vigilant about the interaction of wave energy deployment with the opinions of . . . specific stakeholder groups.

There is a need for wave energy developers now and into the future to be vigilant about the interaction of wave energy deployment with the opinions of the general public and of specific stakeholder groups. It is important not to assume that moving renewable energy offshore guarantees that conflict will automatically be averted. Action must be taken to identify potential sources of conflict as early as possible and to move to come to mutually agreeable solutions which both recognise the needs of established stakeholders as well as allowing the increased deployment of renewable energy technologies with the potential for environmental and other benefits they offer. Lessons may be learned from some of the work that has been done concerning inclusion of different stakeholders and public accountability with regard to other renewable energy technologies, most notably onshore wind energy.

There is considerable work to be done in assessing the ways in which groups and individuals form opinions of wave energy and its potential future role within society.

Putting Results in the Proper Context

There is a need for both greater research into the full impacts of wave energy devices and efforts to more widely promulgate results in the proper context. While environmental impacts are not fully understood either qualitatively or quantitatively then there is potential for gaps in knowledge to be exploited by opponents of the technology or of its particular use. Work needs to be carried out to increase the accuracy of models for impacts of wave energy devices, including at the shoreline, but data alone do not resolve issues of public opinion and public acceptability.

There is considerable work to be done in assessing the ways in which groups and individuals form opinions of wave energy and its potential future role within society. This will need to take place within the greater debate as to how nations address climate change. It will need to be informed by more advanced and complex models for assessment of the physical impacts of wave energy installations as well as of the social and economic implications, both positive and negative. It has become apparent from research in the acceptability of onshore wind energy that much can be done to increase stakeholder trust by inclusion of key representatives at all stages of projects with potential impacts on a stakeholder group. While lessons may be learned from the ways in which support for social and cultural impacts has been applied to other renewable energy technologies, but the particularities of wave [energy technology] would best be served by specific consideration as well as these general conclusions.

11

Federal and State Governments Should Support Tidal Power

Larry Eisenstat and Bethany Dukes

Larry Eisenstat is the head of the energy practice of Dickstein Shapiro LLP, a corporate law firm. Bethany Dukes is an associate at Dickstein Shapiro LLP.

If tidal power is to become a viable commercial alternative energy resource, federal and state governments must provide the same kind of economic stimulation once used to support wind and nuclear power and fossil fuels. Tidal power is emission-free, predictable, and renewable. Although an untested industry, tidal power nevertheless shows promise, despite skepticism that it is not competitive with other energy resources. Federal and state funding would give this fledgling industry a chance to prove itself. Indeed, the Federal Energy Regulatory Commission has helped by expediting permit procedures to lessen some of the burden faced by new tidal power projects.

Hydrokinetic power harnesses the motion of waves or the flow of tides, ocean currents or inland waterways to generate electricity without the impoundments or diversions used in traditional hydropower. Its proponents are quick to extol its many apparent virtues.

Larry Eisenstat and Bethany Dukes, "Overcoming Boundaries (Real and Imagined) to Hydrokinetic Power Development," *Electric Light & Power*, vol. 87, November 1, 2009. Copyright © 2009 PennWell Corporation. Reproduced by permission.

Like other renewable power sources, hydrokinetic projects are renewable, emission-free and virtually silent. They create green jobs for local communities and decrease reliance on oil and natural gas.

Unlike most intermittent resources, waves and tides are predictable. Many projects could be sited near load centers and integrated into the existing electrical system without major expansions. Some East Coast projects might even unload certain transmission facilities, reduce congestion and alleviate part of the need for future transmission lines.

And, if offshore, they would be virtually invisible from the mainland. While many of the more impressive tidal ranges are located abroad, some speculate that the United States alone has enough wave and tidal resource potential to meet about 10 percent of its energy demand.

Finally, the technical risk is becoming increasingly acceptable. The United Kingdom has been promoting hydrokinetic power for some time and in May 2008 connected the first tidal turbine to its grid. The results to date are encouraging.

Federal and state governments must continue providing to hydrokinetic power development the same degree of seed money and other economic stimuli used to advance wind, nuclear, oil and gas.

There also is considerable skepticism [about] whether hydrokinetic power could be cost-competitive and developed on a scale necessary to significantly contribute to the U.S. energy portfolio. Developers first must be willing to sign on to a technology that, while showing significant promise, has yet to be tested over multiple years. Scarce operational data exist concerning its performance, environmental impacts and costs. On its face, it would appear to entail potentially complex installation and maintenance issues. It is reasonable to assume that permitting would be just as lengthy and uncertain, and the difficulties in raising capital would be at least as large, as those faced by more conventional power technologies. Perhaps this is why only two projects have been successfully licensed in the United States.

A Bright Future

Things might be changing, however. While the first federally licensed hydrokinetic project in the United States commenced commercial operation on Aug. 20, [2009,] other projects successfully have completed the demonstration phase and are nearing full-scale implementation, and new projects continue to be developed. More than 140 preliminary permits have been issued for projects that potentially could produce thousands of megawatts. The Federal Energy Regulatory Commission (FERC) has further contributed by developing expedited procedures to lessen the burden on pilot projects seeking these preliminary permits. Together with the Department of the Interior's Mineral Management Service (MMS), it recently streamlined the process of obtaining FERC licenses and leases from MMS for projects on the outer continental shelf. Likewise, states are beginning to coordinate their permitting and leasing processes with the federal licensing process.

Future prospects also appear bright. Arizona Sen[ator] Jeff Bingaman's energy bill provides funding for hydrokinetic energy research and development. In August [2009], the Department of Energy selected several national laboratory-led advanced water power projects to receive up to $11 million in funding, and in September it announced an additional $14.6 million for 22 projects to promote advanced hydropower technologies. In June, President Barack Obama established an interagency Ocean Policy Task Force to develop a cohesive national policy and coordinate state and federal efforts for the nation's oceans.

One must look only to the 1980's wind power development to see why hydrokinetic power is far from dead in the water and what this nascent technology requires to attain the commercial viability and public support that wind power enjoys today.

In light of its technical promise and today's environmental and national security imperatives—and until further development would not make sense—the federal and state governments must continue providing to hydrokinetic power development the same degree of seed money and other economic stimuli used to advance wind, nuclear, oil and gas in the form of direct grants, tax incentives, geologic and meteorologic research or set asides.

12

The Government Should Remove Regulatory Obstacles to Tidal Energy

Jonathan H. Adler

Jonathan H. Adler is a professor at Case Western Reserve University School of Law and director of the Center for Business Law & Regulation. He is a regular contributor to National Review online.

Renewable energy development such as offshore wind farms and tidal power projects often face considerable regulatory obstacles, particularly when developers propose these projects in the backyard of well-funded opposition. Developers of a tidal power project planned in New York's East River have spent at least $7 million to meet state and federal regulatory requirements. The government designed existing rules to regulate traditional power sources, not emerging technologies. If governments want to promote clean, renewable alternative energy resources such as tidal power, they should at least reduce the regulatory burden so that renewable energy entrepreneurs can compete.

Several years ago, Cape Wind Associates proposed the nation's first offshore windfarm in Nantucket Sound [off Massachusetts]. They sought to build 130 wind turbines several miles off the coast on Horseshoe Shoal. The Sound is an ideal location for offshore wind production. The surrounding land masses and relatively shallow water would protect the installation from storms and make it easier to erect and maintain the 258-foot turbine towers. Upon completion, the wind farm could provide approximately 75-percent of Cape Cod's electricity, reducing the need to rely on nearby fossil-fuel-fired power plants. As good as it sounds, the project faces strong opposition.

Well-Funded Opposition

Some local residents and vacation property owners, including the Kennedy family, were outraged at the idea of a wind farm in Nantucket Sound. The prospect of wind turbines dotting the horizon was too much to bear, so they swung into action, launching local p.r. [public relations] campaigns and filing suit to prevent the Cape Wind project's completion. Walter Cronkite [a former broadcast journalist], who owns a home in nearby Martha's Vineyard, warned of an "industrial energy complex" despoiling the "publicly owned" Nantucket Sound. Noted environmental activist Robert F. Kennedy Jr., who has stridently condemned fossil fuel energy production, echoed this concern, decrying plans to soil the "wilderness" of the sound for "industrial development."

Cape Wind's primary opponent, the Alliance to Protect Nantucket Sound, is bankrolled by many wealthy Cape Cod residents and owners of vacation homes, and has spent millions to defeat the campaign—$15 million by one estimate, and $2.4 million in 2003 alone. Though the Alliance has the support of several thousand locals, a few dozen wealthy residents are responsible for the bulk of its financial support. Over three-quarters of the Alliance's funding came from just 56 individuals in 2003.

Cape Wind opponents have raised substantial funds for their campaign, but it is not clear they really speak for local residents, and they certainly do not represent popular opinion within the state. One recent survey found that a majority of locals support the project, and over 80-percent support it statewide. Still the project faces tough sledding. In 2002, federal regulators predicted it would take 18 months to three years for the project to gain approval, yet, as of late 2007, Cape Wind is still yet to begin operation. If the project is approved next year, as some expect, litigation is almost sure to follow, and could delay construction past 2010.

Executives [of one tidal power project] estimate they have spent at least $7 million over seven years working their way through state and federal regulatory requirements.

Stalling Renewable Projects

Cape Wind's opponents have sought to take advantage of various state and federal regulatory requirements to stall the project. These processes create substantial opportunities for activists and NIMBYs ["not in my backyard" opponents] to gum up the works, spurring delays and hoping to scare off investors. Cape Wind's consultants spent four years on a 3,800-page environmental impact statement, but this was not enough to ensure a go. While the project eventually obtained state approval, the federal government has yet to give the final okay.

If pre-existing regulatory requirements were not enough, [Massachusetts] Senator Edward Kennedy conspired with other Senators to enact additional legal obstacles to Cape Wind, burdening all proposed offshore wind power projects in the process. Despite his best efforts, Kennedy failed to kill the project outright, but Cape Wind is still not in the clear—and if Cape Wind fails, the prospects for other offshore wind farms could fall with it.

Cape Wind is hardly the only wind power project to face opposition. Even land-based wind farms have sparked opposition. Local activists are against the erection of additional wind turbines in California's San Gorgonio Pass. In addition to aesthetic concerns, some environmentalists fear wind turbines could harm local bird populations. Feared threats to bird populations were enough to defeat a small wind farm plan in Tennessee.

Local landowners also fought wind turbines on Maine's Beaver Ridge and in western Maryland. In just the past few months, proposed wind farm projects have been scuttled in Texas and New York. Prospects seem brighter for a proposed wind farm off Rehoboth Beach, Delaware, so long as the proposed project is cut down to size. Activists swear they are not opposed to wind power, as such, just the specific wind projects at issue. For many, wind power is a great idea, so long as it is sited in someone else's neighborhood.

Regulatory Obstacles

Wind power is also not the only alternative energy source to face regulatory obstacles and NIMBY opposition. Proposed tidal power projects are having similar experiences with the regulatory process. The Electric Power Research Institute estimates tidal and wave-based energy could provide up to ten percent of the nation's electricity some day. Yet while there are a handful of such facilities overseas, there are none in the United States—at least not yet. The nation's first commercial wave-energy project—a small, one megawatt facility in Washington State—should come on line in Washington State in 2009.

Water-based projects . . . face an array of overlapping, and not always clear, regulatory requirements.

One tidal power project that has received significant attention is Verdant Power's plan for the Big Apple [New York City]. Verdant wants to harness non-polluting tidal power in New York's East River, but it too faces regulatory hurdles. Verdant executives estimate they have spent at least $7 million over seven years working their way through state and federal regulatory requirements. Even a pilot project designed to test turbine design and develop project parameters required permission from the Federal Energy Regulatory Commission, which plans to regulate underwater power generation the same way it regulates large hydroelectric dams. As *The Economist* reported, "this tiny project faces as big a regulatory burden from federal authorities as a giant conventional power station."

Water-based projects, whether they draw power from tides or winds, face an array of overlapping, and not always clear, regulatory requirements. Many of these rules were developed with traditional power sources in mind. In some cases, review processes were adopted to facilitate activist opposition. The end result is that a modest wind farm or potential tide-power operation can be just as vulnerable to obstruction and delay as a major coal facility or hydroelectric dam. Such renewable power facilities have environmental impacts of their own, to be sure. Yet, in most instances their impact will be significantly less than the power sources they displace.

The best thing the federal government can do is reduce or remove regulatory obstacles to energy entrepreneurship and innovation.

A Level Playing Field

Alternative energy advocates often bemoan the lack of a "level playing field" for renewable energy, recommending additional federal subsidies as the solution. Yet renewable energy sources already receive generous financial support from the Department of Energy and other government sources. In practice, such funding does little to bring commercially viable facilities on line.

To promote alternative energy development, there's no need for more handouts. Instead the government should get out of the way. If the goal is to increase actual alternative energy production, and increase the proportion of renewable energy that supplies electricity to American consumers, the best thing the federal government can do is reduce or remove regulatory obstacles to energy entrepreneurship and innovation. If renewable energies are to capture a sizable share of the energy market, what they need, more than anything else, is regulatory room to compete.

13

U.S. Energy Regulations Can Adapt to Ocean Power Technologies

Ann F. Miles

Ann F. Miles is director of the Division of Hydropower Licensing at the Federal Energy Regulatory Commission (FERC), an independent agency whose mandate is to regulate the interstate transmission of electricity, natural gas, and oil. FERC also licenses hydropower projects.

New technologies, including wave and tidal power, could increase hydropower energy production in the United States to 20 percent; however, the commercial development of these new energy technologies is in its infancy. Nevertheless, the Federal Energy Regulatory Commission's (FERC's) existing process is flexible enough to regulate these new energy technologies, consider the interests of stakeholders, and protect the environment. The three-stage process—preliminary permits, licensing, and project compliance—has been continuously refined and is well established. Moreover, FERC has shown that it is flexible enough to respond to new hydropower technologies. For example, FERC allowed Verdant Power to install its experimental tidal turbines in New York's East River without a license so that Verdant could test the turbines and monitor their environmental impact. Indeed, FERC hopes to reduce regulatory barriers for new hydropower technologies where possible.

Ann F. Miles, testimony before the Subcommittee on Fisheries, Wildlife and Oceans and the Subcommittee on Energy and Mineral Resources, Committee on Natural Resources, U.S. House of Representatives, Hearing on Renewable Energy Opportunities and Issues on the Outer Continental Shelf, April 24, 2007. www.ferc.gov.

The [Federal Energy Regulatory] Commission [FERC] regulates over 1,600 hydroelectric projects at over 2,000 dams pursuant to Part I of the Federal Power Act (FPA). Together, these projects represent 57 gigawatts of hydroelectric capacity, more than half of all the hydropower in the United States, and over five percent of all electric generating capacity in the United States. Hydropower is an essential part of the Nation's energy mix and offers the benefits of an emission-free, renewable, domestic energy source with public and private capacity together totaling about ten percent of U.S. capacity. Today we are looking at development of a new source of hydropower that has the potential to add a substantial amount of power to the nation's generation capacity, particularly in the area of renewable energy.

The Commission's existing procedures are well established and well suited to address this expansion of conventional hydropower with new technologies, and we are prepared to learn from experience in this rapidly evolving area and to make whatever regulatory adjustments are appropriate in order to help realize the potential of this renewable energy resource. . . .

Ocean-Based Hydropower Technology

In the past, efficient and reliable conversion of kinetic energy from water has proven elusive, but with recent advances in technology, rising fuel costs, and a growing demand for renewable energy, the potential for hydropower using new technologies is on the rise. An Electrical Power Research Institute (EPRI) study estimated the potential for wave and current power in our nation's oceans to be over 350 billion kilowatt hours per year, which would equal the output of traditional hydropower in its most productive years. In other words, ocean-based hydropower using new technologies could double hydropower production going from 10 to 20% of the national total. At present, however, the development and commercialization of the new technologies are just beginning.

The wave energy technologies include a range of designs including buoys, barge-like devices, and small floating reservoirs. Designs for harnessing tidal and current energy generally are variations on traditional turbines, often using underwater "propellers." In both cases, the energy of the moving water or wave is converted into electricity within each unit, making each device a small powerhouse. The current stage of technological development ranges from concept sketches to pilot demonstration projects.

Wave energy can be harnessed in locations that range from at the shoreline to many miles off shore, while tidal energy is limited to tidal rivers and narrows associated with coastal bays and estuaries, and ocean currents are located mainly in offshore locations such as the Gulf Stream. Tidal power has substantial hourly variations during the day but the pattern tends to be very predictable across seasons and years, while wave power is much steadier on an hourly basis but shows more seasonal variation.

Ultimately, whether the source is wave, tide, or current, it likely will take clusters or fields of devices to generate utility-scale power from the new technologies. The electricity from the devices will in most cases be connected by an underwater cable to the shore and then continue onshore to connect with the interstate transmission grid.

Ocean Energy Activity

Applications for ocean-based hydropower projects can potentially go through three stages at the Commission. First, developers can apply for preliminary permits. Preliminary permits maintain priority of application for license for a site for up to three years while a developer researches site feasibility and makes financial arrangements. Second, developers can apply for a hydropower license. (A preliminary permit is not required prior to applying for a license.) By statute the Commission can issue a license for a term of up to 50 years. Third, if licensed, the developer must operate the project in compliance with the terms of the Commission's license order. Throughout the term of the license, the Commission monitors the project to assure compliance with the license.

Recently, the Commission has seen a surge in applications for preliminary permits for the new technologies. Before 2004, the Commission had received no recent preliminary permit applications for projects using ocean technologies. We received 11 permit applications in calendar years 2004 and 2005 combined and over 40 permit applications in 2006 alone. We have received four more permit applications so far in 2007. In 2005 and 2006, the Commission issued 11 preliminary permits, three for proposed tidal energy projects, and eight for proposed ocean current energy projects. So far in 2007, the Commission [has] issued 19 permits, 16 for proposed tidal energy projects and three for proposed ocean wave energy projects.

The Commission received the first license application for a wave energy hydropower project from AquaEnergy, Inc. in November 2006. The Makah Bay Offshore Wave Energy Project is proposed for Makah Bay in Clallam County, Washington. Part of the project would be located on lands of the Makah Nation Indian Reservation. The project would consist of four buoys moored 3.2 nautical miles offshore in the Olympic Coast National Marine Sanctuary. Together, the buoys would generate up to 1 megawatt (MW), with an average of about 200 kilowatts (kW), through relative motion created by waves, which drives an internal pump that would force pressurized water through a closed-loop hose and a turbine.

In the tidal hydropower arena, Commission staff has been working with Verdant Power, LLC, a permit holder seeking to develop a license application for the Roosevelt Island Tidal Energy Hydropower Project. The project ultimately would consist of as many as 494 free-flowing turbine generator units (about 10.3 MW total), located below the water surface in the East River in Queens County, New York. . . .

The Commission's Existing Process

Projects using new technologies are compatible with the Commission's well-tested regulatory process that has been refined continuously since the original passage of the Federal Water Power Act of 1920. Regulating the development of power generation from the nation's waters is a primary role of the Commission. We analyze developers' proposals for energy generation from navigable and Commerce Clause waters, along with interests expressed by other stakeholders, and comprehensively balance the benefit of power generation with environmental protection and other values as directed by statute. After years of collaboration with other agencies and parties we have achieved a high level of regulatory efficiency. Over the years, we have improved our licensing process to include early engagement with the applicant and other stakeholders, earlier and more predictable study requirements, more certain timeframes, and overall reduced processing time.

Regulatory Flexibility

In reviewing a license application for a project, the Commission integrates and weighs the concerns of the licensee, federal and state resource agencies, tribes, and other members of the public. We do so through an information-gathering process and technical analysis that enables a fully informed Commission decision while complying with the mandates of the Federal Power Act, the National Environmental Policy Act, the Endangered Species Act, and other applicable laws.

Within our established process, significant flexibility exists to implement innovative approaches when appropriate. For instance, in the Makah Bay and Roosevelt Island cases, Commission staff has allowed the use of different license processes that better fit the applicants' needs. This flexibility has enabled 1) the inclusion of Commission staff and stakeholders in the study development and implementation and 2) for much of the National Environmental Policy Act [NEPA] information to be developed parallel to the project's license application development. In the Roosevelt Island case, the process may also encourage negotiation of a settlement.

Improving Compatibility

Where the needs of the industry have raised new issues, not within the scope of our standard procedures, the Commission has shown the maximum flexibility allowed by the statute. For example, the Commission determined that Verdant Power could install its six-turbine demonstration project in the East River without applying for a Commission license. In a July 27, 2005, Order on Clarification, the Commission concluded that Verdant's activities effectively would have no net impact on the interstate electric power grid or on interstate commerce. This determination established a policy that allows experimentation without a license when 1) the technology in question is experimental; 2) the proposed facilities are to be used for a short period and for the purpose of developing a hydropower license application; and 3) power generated from the test project will not be transmitted into, or displaced from, the national electric energy grid. In addition to testing power generation, Verdant will carry out extensive monitoring of fishery impacts as part of the experimental deployment. Although not required to be licensed during its testing phase, Verdant was of course obligated to obtain necessary approvals under other existing state and federal statutes. . . .

In the area of licensing, the Commission staff considers our well-tested existing procedures to work well, yet to be sufficiently flexible to address the licensing of projects using the new technologies. Where appropriate, Commission staff will investigate making improvements to the current process to the extent consistent with existing law. We will continue to use our substantial experience and expertise in bringing other agencies together in determining appropriate studies and complying with all existing statutes and to make the regulatory process for agencies, applicants, and parties as efficient as possible. To address a concern about a lack of information about the environmental effects of these technologies, Commission staff has been gathering information and studies on the environmental effects of ocean energy and, in coordination with other agencies, will be making this information available as a service to developers as well as using it to accelerate our reviews. We also plan to provide outreach on our program to clarify our process for the industry and stakeholders, many of whom are new to it. . . .

Projects using new technologies are compatible with the [Federal Energy Regulatory] Commission's well-tested regulatory process.

I am happy to report that the two agencies [FERC and the Department of the Interior] are working together to develop a Memorandum of Agreement that will apply the best resources and authorities of both agencies to develop an efficient and effective program for promoting and regulating the development of hydropower in all offshore areas, including the OCS [Outer Continental Shelf]. We believe that the Commission brings several resources to the negotiating table. First, the Commission is uniquely positioned under the FPA and its regulations to give equal consideration to developmental and non-developmental resources and to assure that any project licensed will be best adapted to a comprehensive plan for development of the water resource in the public interest. Second, the Commission has many years experience in hydropower licensing. The Commission's licensing process is transparent, provides timely review of projects, and affords applicants, agencies, Native American Tribes, Non-governmental organizations and members of the public numerous opportunities to effectively participate and represent their interests.

Consulting with State and Federal Agencies

State and other federal agencies (agencies) play a central role in the Commission's existing hydropower licensing process. This role will continue to be essential as we address the new hydropower technologies. The National Marine Fisheries Service (NMFS) within the National Oceanic and Atmospheric Administration of the U.S. Department of Commerce is one of the federal agencies that has been actively involved in the Commission's licensing process for conventional hydropower projects and we expect that they would be similarly involved in new technology projects. The Commission staff works closely with the agencies to address their interests and concerns and to tap their expertise with "on the ground" management of the resource. Cooperation and consultation with the agencies begins early in application development and continues throughout the licensing process.

The Commission requires that applicants consult with agencies in the process of preparing an application. The application must include the results of this consultation with a description of agency recommendations and the applicant's response to the recommendations. The Commission's Integrated Licensing Process regulations require early involvement of Commission staff in pre-application phase discussions with agencies and the applicant. The process includes a formal procedure for consulting with the agencies to determine the studies needed for licensing and includes both an informal and formal dispute resolution process. Under the Federal Power Act, Congress assigned the state and federal fish and wildlife agencies specific authority in hydropower licensing. Essentially, the Commission is to accept state and federal fish and wildlife agency recommendations unless they clearly are in conflict with another part of the statute. These recommendations contribute to the comprehensive balancing of energy development and the protection of fish, wildlife, recreation, and other resources. Finally, the Commission's licensing process and supporting analysis incorporates other statutes in which Congress has given important authorities to the states, such as the Coastal Zone Management Act of 1972 and the National Historic Preservation Act of 1966. Together, these statutory, regulatory, and informal relationships have supported good coordination and cooperation with the states that will extend to the new technologies.

Under the [Federal Energy Regulatory] Commission's statutory structure, . . . hydropower resources using new technologies can be developed in an orderly way while protecting other beneficial public uses.

In addition, Section 10(a)(2)(A) of the FPA authorizes states and federal agencies to file Comprehensive Plans that address one or more beneficial uses of a waterway. The Commission takes these Comprehensive Plans into account when determining whether and under what conditions a project should be licensed. These plans enable state and federal agencies to have a substantial role in the Commission's public interest determination.

Finally, I would suggest that the Commission's many years of experience in analyzing the environmental effects of hydropower projects under existing statutes, including NEPA, and implementing regulations provide an ample foundation to adequately address the environmental effects of new technology projects.

Helping Promote a Promising Renewable Resource

In closing, the Commissioners have stated publicly their interest in promoting the development of this potentially important source of renewable energy. They also have expressed their desire to reduce regulatory barriers to the development of new technologies, where possible.

We are confident that under the Commission's statutory structure, refined over almost a century, hydropower resources using new technologies can be developed in an orderly way while protecting other beneficial public uses, such as fish and wildlife, and meeting the requirements of other federal statutes and state interests. As experience is gained in the area of new hydropower technologies, we will make appropriate regulatory adjustments as we have in response to other technology changes in the past. We will work with the Minerals Management Service to develop a program for the OCS that makes the best and most efficient use of our respective resources and provides thorough analysis of environmental impacts, and we will continue to cooperate and consult with other federal agencies, including NMFS, and individual states in the licensing of new technology projects. We look forward to continuing to carry out the Congressional mandate in the Federal Power Act and performing our regulatory duties fairly, openly, and efficiently to realize the potential of this promising renewable energy resource.

Organizations to Contact

The editors have compiled the following list of organizations concerned with the issues debated in this book. The descriptions are derived from materials provided by the organizations. All have publications or information available for interested readers. The list was compiled on the date of publication of the present volume; the information provided here may change. Be aware that many organizations take several weeks or longer to respond to inquiries, so allow as much time as possible.

Electric Power Research Institute (EPRI)
3420 Hillview Ave., Palo Alto, CA 94304
(800) 313-3774
e-mail: askepri@epri.com
Web site: http://my.epri.com

EPRI is an independent, nonprofit center that conducts research on the generation, delivery, and use of electricity for public benefit. EPRI brings together scientists and engineers as well as experts from academia and industry to help address electricity challenges, including reliability, efficiency, health, safety, and the environment. The *EPRI Journal* reports on and provides insight into energy issues, including wave and tidal power. Reports about ocean wave and tidal renewable energy are available on EPRI's Web site, including *Ocean Tidal and Wave Energy: Renewable Energy Technical Assessment*, *Ocean Energy Technologies: The State of the Art*, and *Hawaii Ocean Current Resources and Tidal Turbine Assessment*.

Environmental and Energy Study Institute (EESI)
1112 Sixteenth St. NW, Suite 300
Washington, DC 20036-4819
(202) 628-1400 • fax: (202) 204-5244
Web site: www.eesi.org

EESI is a nonprofit organization established by Congress in 1984 to provide timely information and develop innovative policy solutions that set the United States on a cleaner, more secure, and sustainable energy path. EESI accomplishes these objectives by educating policy makers, improving communication among stakeholders, and developing policy. The institute publishes issue and policy papers as well as a newsletter. The report, *The Role of Advanced Hydropower and Ocean Energy in Upcoming Energy Legislation* is available on EESI's Web site.

Environmental Defense Fund
257 Park Ave. South, New York, NY   10010
(212) 505-2100
Web site: www.environmentaldefense.org

Founded by scientists in 1967, the Environmental Defense Fund conducts original research and enlists outside experts to solve environmental problems. The advocacy group forms partnerships with corporations to promote environmentally friendly business practices. On its Web site, the fund publishes news, fact sheets, reports, and articles, including "Wave and Tidal Power: Energy from the Seas" and "Ocean Renewable Energy: A Shared Vision and Call for Action."

European Marine Energy Centre (EMEC)
Old Academy, Back Rd., Stromness, Orkney   KW16 3AW
   United Kingdom
+44 (0) 1856 852060
Web site: www.emec.org.uk

EMEC is a research center focusing on wave and tidal power development based in the Orkney Islands, United Kingdom. This location provides developers with the opportunity to test full-scale, grid-connected prototype devices in unrivaled wave and tidal conditions. The organization was established in 2001 following a recommendation by the House of Commons Science and Technology Committee. EMEC also offers support regarding regulatory issues, grid connection, meteorological monitoring, research, and engineering.

European Ocean Energy Association (EU-OEA)
Renewable Energy House, Rue d'Arlon 63–65
Brussels   B-1040
  Belgium
+32 (0)2 400 10 40
e-mail: secretariat@eu-oea.com
Web site: www.eu-oea.com

EU-OEA unites the interests of the European ocean energy industry into a single voice. With regional and industry partners, EU-OEA members address issues of relevance to the industry with regulators, legislators, and policy makers. On its Web site, within the technology link, which is located within the association's ocean energy link, EU-OEA explores various wave and tidal power technologies.

Federal Energy Regulatory Commission (FERC)
888 First St. NE, Washington, DC   20426
(866) 208-3372
e-mail: customer@ferc.gov
Web site: www.ferc.gov

FERC is an independent agency that regulates the interstate transmission of electricity, natural gas, and oil. FERC also reviews proposals to build liquefied natural gas (LNG) terminals and interstate natural gas pipelines and licenses hydropower projects, including hydrokinetic projects—those that generate electricity from waves or directly from the flow of water in ocean currents, tides, or inland waterways. FERC's mission is to ensure that consumers obtain reliable, efficient, and sustainable energy services at a reasonable cost through appropriate regulatory and market means.

Hydropower Reform Coalition
1101 Fourteenth St. NW, Suite 1400, Washington, DC   20005
(202) 243-7076 • fax: (202) 347-9240
Web site: www.hydroreform.org/

Founded in 1992 as a loose association of conservation and recreation groups, the Hydropower Reform Coalition has grown into a broad consortium of more than 140 national, regional, and local organizations with a combined membership of more than 1 million people. The coalition has protected or restored thousands of river miles, thousands of acres of watershed land, and countless opportunities for boating, fishing, and other forms of recreation. On its Web site, the coalition's Policy Watch link updates readers on hydropower issues, including recent news concerning wave and tidal power projects.

National Hydropower Association (NHA)
25 Massachusetts Ave. NW, Suite 340, Washington, DC   20001
(202) 682-1700 • fax: (202) 682-9478
e-mail: help@hydro.org
Web site: www.hydro.org

The NHA is a nonprofit national association dedicated to advancing the interests of the hydropower industry. It seeks to secure hydropower's place as a climate friendly, renewable, and reliable energy source that serves national environmental and energy policy objectives. On its Web site, the NHA publishes fact sheets, issue briefs, and white papers about hydropower issues, including wave and tidal energy, such as "Wave Energy—The Next Step for Renewable Energy."

National Renewable Energy Laboratory (NREL)
1617 Cole Blvd., Golden, CO   80401-3393
(303) 275-3000
Web site: www.nrel.gov

NREL is the nation's primary laboratory for renewable energy and energy efficiency research and development. NREL's mission is to develop renewable energy and energy efficiency technologies to address the nation's energy and environmental goals. NREL works to bring new renewable energy technologies from the laboratory to the marketplace. The agency publishes *Discover NREL*, a bimonthly newsletter. On its Web site, NREL provides a student resource page and publishes reports on renewable technologies, including "Status of Wave and Tidal Power Technologies for the United States."

Natural Resources Defense Council (NRDC)
40 W. Twentieth St., New York, NY   10011
(212) 727-2700
e-mail: proinfo@nrdc.org
Web site: www.nrdc.org

The NRDC is a nonprofit organization that uses both law and science to protect the planet's wildlife and wild places and to ensure a safe and healthy environment for all living things. The NRDC publishes the quarterly magazine *OnEarth* and the bimonthly bulletin *Nature's Voice*. On its Web site NRDC provides links to specific environmental topics and news, articles, and reports, including "Third Time's a Charm for NYC Tidal Power."

**Northwest National Marine Renewable
Energy Center (NNMREC)**
University of Washington, Box 352600
Seattle, WA   98195-2600
(206) 909-1771 • fax: (206) 685-8047
Web site: http://nnmrec.oregonstate.edu/about

NNMREC is a partnership between Oregon State University and the University of Washington. The role of the center is to close key gaps in understanding of marine energy and to inform the public, regulators, research institutions, and device and site developers. Oregon State University focuses on wave energy. The University of Washington focuses on tidal energy. Both universities collaborate with each other and the National Renewable Energy Laboratory on research, education, outreach, and engagement. Information on tidal and wave energy are available on NNMREC's Web sites.

Ocean Energy Council
11985 Southern Blvd., Suite 155, West Palm Beach, FL   33411
(561) 795-0320 • fax: (561) 795-5087
e-mail: info@oceanenergycouncil.com
Web site: www.oceanenergycouncil.com

The Ocean Energy Council is a nonprofit organization whose mission is to improve public knowledge and acceptance of ocean energy as a viable resource with its own special advantages, ranking with oil, natural gas, nuclear power, coal, and direct solar applications in contributing to the national and international energy supply. The council makes recommendations to the U.S. Department of Energy and other governmental bodies; fosters educational advancement and growth of members in the field of ocean energy; educates the public on the potential and current status of development of ocean energy; and engages with groups, organizations, and other bodies whose purposes include the implementation of environmentally friendly alternative energy sources. On its Web site, the council publishes information on wave and tidal energy technologies and projects.

Property and Environment Research Center (PERC)
2048 Analysis Dr., Suite A, Bozeman, MT   59718
(406) 587-9591
e-mail: perc@perc.org
Web site: www.perc.org

PERC is a nonprofit research and educational organization that seeks market-oriented solutions to environmental problems. The center holds a variety of conferences and provides educational material. It publishes the quarterly newsletter *PERC Reports*, commentaries, research studies, and policy papers, many of which are available on its Web site, including "Riding the Waves."

Surfrider Foundation
PO Box 6010, San Clemente, CA   92674-6010
(949) 492-8170 • fax: (949) 492-8142
Web site: www.surfrider.org

Founded in 1984 by a handful of visionary surfers in Malibu, California, the Surfrider Foundation is a nonprofit grassroots organization dedicated to the protection and enjoyment of the world's oceans, waves, and beaches. The foundation recognizes that technologies that utilize ocean waves, tides, currents, and wind may offer important benefits as renewable energy sources that will reduce greenhouse gas emissions and provide economic development for coastal communities. Surfrider also recognizes, however, that there are many questions and concerns about ocean energy, including potential environmental, economic, and recreational impacts. The foundation therefore works to ensure that energy generated from ocean resources meets objectives consistent with its mission. The foundation publishes the bimonthly *Making Waves* magazine and the *State of the Beach* report.

Union of Concerned Scientists (UCS)
2 Brattle Sq., Cambridge, MA   02238
(617) 547-5552 • fax: (617) 864-9405
e-mail: ucs@ucsusa.org
Web site: www.ucsusa.org

The Union of Concerned Scientists aims to advance responsible public policy in areas where science and technology play important roles. Its programs emphasize transportation reform, arms control, safe and renewable energy technologies, and sustainable agriculture. The organization's publications include the twice-yearly magazine *Catalyst*, the quarterly newsletter *Earthwise*, and the electronic newsletter *Greentips*. Recent issues of its publications are available on its Web site, including the article "Wave Power Generation." The union's Clean Energy link includes information on how hydrokinetic energy works.

Worldwatch Institute
1776 Massachusetts Ave. NW, Washington, DC   20036-1904
(202) 452-1999 • fax: (202) 296-7365
e-mail: worldwatch@worldwatch.org
Web site: www.worldwatch.org

Worldwatch is a nonprofit public policy research organization dedicated to informing the public and policy makers about emerging global problems and trends and the complex links between the environment and the world economy. Its publications include *Vital Signs*, issued every year, the *Environmental Alert* series, numerous policy papers and reports, and the bimonthly magazine *World Watch*, which includes the article "Ocean Motion Power."

Bibliography

Books

Don Baur, Tim Eichenberg, and G. Michael Sutton, eds.
Ocean and Coast Law and Policy. Chicago: American Bar Association, 2008.

Godfrey Boyle
Renewable Energy: Power for a Sustainable Future. New York: Oxford University Press, 2004.

Roger Henri Charlier and Charles W. Finkl
Ocean Energy: Tide and Tidal Power. London: Springer, 2008.

Robert H. Clark
Elements of Tidal-Electric Engineering. Hoboken, NJ: Wiley/IEEE Press, 2007.

Joãto Cruz, ed.
Ocean Wave Energy: Current Status and Future Perspectives. Berlin: Springer, 2008.

Aldo V. da Rosa
Fundamentals of Renewable Energy Processes. Boston: Elsevier, 2009.

Engineering Committee on Oceanic Resources, Working Group on Wave Energy Conversion
Wave Energy Conversion. New York: Elsevier, 2003.

| Johannes Falnes | *Ocean Waves and Oscillating Systems.* New York: Cambridge University Press, 2002. |

Jack Hardisty | *The Analysis of Tidal Stream Power.* Hoboken, NJ: Wiley, 2009.

Martin Kaltschmitt, Wolfgang Streicher, and Andreas Wiese | *Renewable Energy: Technology, Economics, and Environment.* New York: Springer, 2007.

Alireza Khaligh and Omer C. Onar | *Energy Harvesting: Solar, Wind, and Ocean Energy Conversion Systems.* Boca Raton, FL: CRC, 2009.

Paul Komor | *Renewable Energy Policy.* Lincoln, NE: iUniverse, 2004.

David J.C. MacKay | *Sustainable Energy—Without the Hot Air.* Cambridge, UK: UIT Cambridge, 2008.

Michael E. McCormick | *Ocean Wave Energy Conversion.* Mineola, NY: Dover, 2007.

Lynne Peppas | *Ocean, Tidal, and Wave Energy: Power from the Sea.* New York: Crabtree, 2008.

Mike Robinson | *Ocean Energy Technology Development.* Golden, CO: National Renewable Energy Laboratory, 2006.

Ted Trainer | *Renewable Energy Cannot Sustain a Consumer Society.* London: Springer, 2007.

| John Twidell and Tony Weir | *Renewable Energy Resources.* New York: Taylor & Francis, 2006. |
| Roland Wengenmayr and Thomas Bührke, eds. | *Renewable Energy: Sustainable Energy Concepts for the Future.* Hoboken, NJ: Wiley, 2008. |

Periodicals

Thomas F. Armistead	"Wave and Tidal Generation Open a New Frontier for Renewables," *ENR: Engineering News-Record*, May 14, 2007.
Colin Barras	"The Limited Life Span of Wave Powers Wonderful Creatures," *New Scientist*, March 6, 2010.
Barbara Barrett	"U.S. Explores Ocean Winds, Waves, Currents as New Energy Sources," *McClatchy Newspapers*, November 5, 2007.
Les Blumenthal	"Hurdle for Renewable Tidal Power," *Tacoma (WA) News Tribune*, May 31, 2009.
Larissa Curlik	"Stormy Seas: Ocean Power Promoters Struggle to Overcome a Stiff Current of Challenges," *Earth Island Journal*, Spring 2009.
Sandy Doughton	"Tapping Tidal Energy: The Wave of the Future," *Seattle Times*, October 7, 2007.

Economist	"Tapping the Power of the Sea," April 28, 2007.
Economist	"Tidal Power Divides the Greens," January 29, 2009.
Peter Fraenkel	"The Affairs of Tides," *New Scientist*, May 1, 2010.
Magnus Gardham	"Scotland Rules the Waves; Biggest Bid in History to Harness Awesome Power of the Sea," *Daily Record* (Glasgow), March 17, 2010.
Thomas K. Grose	"Surfing Energy's Next Wave," *U.S. News & World Report*, April 1, 2010.
Guardian (Manchester, UK)	"High Water," July 21, 2008.
John Gulland	"Not-So-New Energy Sources Makes Waves," *Mother Earth News*, October/November 2009.
Lee Hibbert	"Sea Change," *Professional Engineering*, February 24, 2010.
David C. Holzman	"Blue Power Turning Tides into Electricity," *Environmental Health Perspectives*, December 2007.
Independent (London)	"The Rise of British Sea Power," March 23, 2008.
Anthony T. Jones and Adam Westwood	"Power from the Oceans," *Futurist*, January/February 2005.

Lisa A. Kelley   "The Power of the Sea: Using Ocean Energy to Meet Florida's Need for Power," *Environmental Law*, Spring 2007.

Margaret Kriz   "Surf Power," *National Journal*, April 28, 2007.

Bret Lortie   "A New Wave of Energy," *Bulletin of the Atomic Scientists*, November/December 2003.

Stephen Morris   "Beyond Fossil Fuels," *New Statesman*, November 30, 2009.

Eric Munday   "Using Sonar to Investigate Interactions Between Marine Life, Subsea Turbines," *Sea Technology*, September 2009.

Natural Life   "Moon Power," January/February 2004.

Ocean News & Technology   "Overcoming Hurdles with Perseverance in Tidal Power," October 2009.

Neal Peirce   "Tapping into Tidal Power," *Seattle Times*, July 31, 2006.

Jeff Postelwait   "Wave and Tidal Power Growing Slowly, Steadily," *Electric Light and Power*, November 2009.

Renewable Energy Focus   "UK Wave and Tidal—Swelling Industry or Risky Business?" March 2010.

Jessica Rettig	"Reality Check: The Powers That Be," *U.S. News & World Report*, April 2010.
Rose Riddell	"Turning Tides," *Engineering & Technology*, September 20–October 3, 2008.
Elizabeth Rusch	"Catching a Wave, Powering an Electrical Grid?" *Smithsonian*, July 2009.
Hans van Haren	"Tidal Power? No Thanks," *New Scientist*, April 3, 2010.

Index